Observations of Life by the Art of Review

Observations of Life by

The Art of Review

Ufi Auttorri

Tam Warink, Editor

Vurmstah
Saint Louis, Missouri **63302**
USA

Vurmstah Press and logo are trademarks of Vurmstah.

Publisher's Cataloging-in-Publication Data

Auttorri, Ufi.
   Observations of Life by The Art of Review by Ufi Auttorri.
   p. cm
   "A Vurmstah Press book."
   ISBN 978-0972472425 (pbk.)
1. Analysis
2. Literature
I. Auttorri, Ufi. II. Title

First published in the United States

Cover concept and illustration by Maurice Rampaux
Cover design by Aunre Pouland

All photography and illustrations in this book were reproduced with the kind permission of their owners, or else are in the public domain.

The sun is fun but the light is too bright!

Anonymous

Contents

I   **Random Consciousness**   **1**

II   **Reviews**   **7**

1   Breathing Trees   9

2   Purple Sticky Notes   17

3   Becalmed Sailor'd Souls   23

4   Smiling Faces   29

5   Godzilla Tsunami   37

6   Love Handles   43

7   Mystery Menus   49

8   Tattered Hats   55

9   Big Dismal Boo Boos   61

10	Reckoning Dust	69
11	Potted Plants	75
12	Sparkling Strings	81
13	Unique Pricks	87
14	Inside Prize	93
15	Whole Halves	99
16	Surviving Tolerance	105
17	Harsh Clarity	111
18	Caring Curves	115
19	Splitting Rails	123
20	Eros Goodbyes	129
21	Buoyant Laughs	137
22	Tetrahedral Firmaments	143
23	Salmon Footprints	151
24	Brave Pens	157
25	Chunking Times	163
26	Invisible Spectrums	173

27 Fluid Definitions   179

28 Pensive Inkdrops   185

29 Redundant Darkness   191

30 Bound Writhing   197

31 Befuddle and Discourage   203

32 Elmo Brainfluff   209

33 Typewriter Brooms   215

34 Velvet Chirps   221

III Review Exercises   229

35 Practice Material   231

36 Poems - I   233

37 Poems - II   259

38 Stories   281

Index   309

Part I

Random
Consciousness

Preface

This book contains selected critiques of poetry and stories by various authors. They were posted in various public online writing websites. It is primarily a collection of random commentary and subjective feedback (critiques, micro-reviews, commentary, blurbs, enthusiasm, pessimism, etc.). They are meant to provide the reader with a few of my observations on life as well as, in the abstract, a primer-by-example on the artistic aspect of review. It is done in a style that is a quasi-literary critique. It's focus is upon the delicate (yet sometimes urbane) virtuosity required to say what one is thinking but in such a way as to leave the recipient of said review with some length of interpretive rope. It is usually sufficient to enable them to do one of two things. Either pull themselves up from the depths of some despair or, often the more likely of the two, give them sufficient opportunity to ponder why it lies coiled tightly about their neck.

At one time I had thought to include the various author's original poems or stories reviewed, as exemplars. I imagined that it might add some clarity and insight for each review offered to authors over the interval of life spanned by this collection. However, in due time, that format was rejected. Mostly because of the great effort that would ensue from seeking copyright and publication permissions from each.

Assume then that each review has an object of interpretive contemplation but know that it has been intentionally omitted for the reason previously mentioned. I confess that I am unabashedly lazy in this respect and apologize if it detracts somewhat from any implicit message or review prose. The original authors will no doubt find my lack of diligence refreshing (or horrifying) as the case may be. It will, I hope, prove a prudent decision.

At present there is no particular ordering to the reviews. They are chosen mostly for their strength of clarity or stylistic demeanor with respect to the finer aspects of the art. If that last statement does not make sense (at the moment) then please have patience. I sincerely hope it will by the time you have finished examining each stream-of-consciousness product.... and they are, indeed, written in a style that could be categorized as such. You will find this thematic approach prevalent throughout and, hopefully, it will not distract too much from the honest intent or well-intentioned advice offered by one that having been so tasked may, at best, be described as a backseat driver or sideline quarterback.

While authors offer up their heart, soul and hours of ceaseless toil (for reasons known only to themselves) we who purvey the art of review bring only a weak broth and a few well-polished stones as guests at that banquet of reflective commiseration. But there is satisfaction to be had by all and we have only to understand that "Beauty beholds itself and knows no other." The savory flavor of truth for this, if not known or understood now, will (I hope) become apparent in due time.

Organizationally speaking there is a certain unnamed grouping for these things; perhaps. I haven't made up my mind yet. However, names of people or authors, things that might provide more than trivial clues to the identification of actual people - these have been replaced with mundane symbolism: XX for female and XY for male. It is intentional. (I have no desire to expend energy entertaining courts of law or debating the laws in courts.)

One final note to all those that would review the reviewer; for each and every defect you may find here, judged by yours or any other standard you may choose, please understand... it is what it was meant to be.

Ufi Auttorri

Lampwick on Melamine, County of St. Louis

Part II

Reviews

Chapter 1

Breathing Trees

When one first finds their "voice" it may often seem to them a bit squeaky and timid. There is too, at times, the almost unbearable imagining that they have exhaled and the words or melody that issue forth seem to gasp for air of their own accord. Others however often perceive it quite differently. To them there is a sense of delicate vibration, of grassy reeds waving, subtly, moved by a steady shoreline breeze. There is an invisible motion of time and space that lays waste to concerns that previously troubled. No longer burdened the soul is freed. It takes wing with a small hopping tilt from the ledge of consciousness and falling briefly then soars toward clouds draped about tree-cloaked mountains where "blissful souls .. surround my table" and "give me the echo of reminiscence."

It is such a difficult thing for the audience, the reader, the recipient of such marvelous constructions to communicate. For in the end there is only applause, perhaps a few exhalations in the style of the period or roses; token gestures that impart little to nothing of the gifts given and received. Yet it is all we, as audience, have and I for one lay them gently at your feet.

When It Rains

"When It Rains..." sometimes I play the cello.

The sound is unusually thick and complaining. When that happens, I imagine it as a viola and I play the upper register harmonics. They are the brighter, more cheerful tones. But a cello is just a cello. It was made to play the low registers and in so doing provide a balance to the overly enthusiastic vibrato of violins and the manic cheerfulness of woodwinds and flutes. Although, in the hands of a master, the cello can be a simulacrum for the somber author smitten with a view from/of the bottom of the abyss.

Conversely, some authors, periodic visitors (or perhaps permanent residents) of the abyss may evoke the harmonies of despair, the melodies of melancholy and the counterpoint of subtle anguish for a libretto of fated lives gone awry; as in this piece. A reader stumbling upon such a work can only wonder, unconsciously perhaps, at the plethora of causalities that provide a portion of the inspiration to manifest such lyric emotion. For all the rationality brought to bear in the assimilation of such lines there is no escaping their rapacious effect. They consume and devour with their serrated perceptions of life in the abyss. A life that is metaphorically strangled into unconsciousness and then revived. Sufficient to suffer again the same cycles of hope and despair.

This piece is all that and more. Here we see a creature of the abyss that has been trawled to the surface in what appears to be an accidental netting; put on display in a special exhibit open to the public for the price of admission. We succumb to the barkers call. The admission is the purchase and the purchase is the admission; or rather the commiseration that is evoked from the viewers that gawk in amazement and titter at how closely a fellow companion resembles the creature from the deep while reluctantly acknowledging their own ancestry and common lineage.

The exit, a queued moment of lined, silent reflection, "How long can it live like that?"

["I have never been depressed a day in my life. I never tell a lie." - The Unborn.]

Dining Dinosloppers

This is all it takes to get them going you know. Someone, you perhaps, describing the situation for them in a way they would have least chosen and in so doing providing them with yet more fodder with which to disassemble and reassemble the problem du jour. I must admit that upon first reading I "heard" and "saw" the words but nothing was being processed. You captured, almost precisely, a lecture that I stumbled into one fine day many, many years ago. It was rather like that. Lovely people, their mouths opening, words coming out, lovely little diagrams appearing on the walls, yet absolutely nothing registering between my ears. My stomach was making more sense. At least it was telling me in no uncertain terms that I had skipped lunch quite unnecessarily. Now, the question remains... do I crown you with laurel or poison ivy? Perhaps I should leave the de-cision in the hands of the X-spurts that know they gnaw on nothing of substance most of the time. What would be your choice?

— *In reply:*

Haha....I knew, I just knew (how did I know?) you'd throw the ball back at me! What would be my choice? A hard one, I think....but probably a no-brainer for me in the end, because I've never been able to explain origin to myself, so remain agnostic. The subject fas-cinates me, always has. Fred Hoyle spent thirty years trying to prove that the universe was self-sustaining, only to have his theory shot down in flames by the scientific establishment, who stopped the start of ex-istence at the Big Bang (this phrase was derogatorily coined by Hoyle) I'm a great Hoyle fan (I read his novel The Black Cloud in my twenties (you'd love it!) If they stick to E=MC squared the Big Bang is were they stop...or rather, start. X.

— *In re-reply:*

I think you're right, X. O'le Fred H. would have been proud of you. After reading that next-to-last stanza for the Umpteenth time, I believe I (finally) have a picture in my head of what you actually said. Oh, and the color of the balloon I used was... what else, RED.

Idle RPMs

A rendering of morality, twisted with a bit of factory fantasy. For me the boat was still moored to the dock; the hawser looped about a pylon. There is a creaking of the deck planks as the engines struggle against the tether of solidly embedded pilings. Those random tourists in pursuit of a weekend away cannot always know what is in store for them. It's usually why they keep to the gift shops and return home with a few curios and a box of sweets. If they knew that the road would be twisted at such angles I wonder if they would have undertaken the journey in the first place? Probably... tourists are crazy like that, aren't they? ☺

Deftly Positioned Gallery Lights

That last line is such a stark postulation, XX. I tried cutting my own hair once but it turned out... well, let's just say it wasn't "gallery quality." So, I took your strategy to heart and kept the shades half drawn because a glimpse of my work would have ruined any possible chance for romance. No, I did not prance in the sunlight but I hope to soon. Perhaps I will find that lost adjective as I dangle my feet in the water and search for a way to complete that unfinished line. Do you think love would help?

Refreshing Draughts

An encouragement and a reason. What more could we ask from those that care? Honest and forthright words always have the possibility of lifting someone up. However, as someone totally NOT famous must have said once, "You can lead a horse to water but you can't make 'em drink." But, thirst, for love, for companionship, for true friendship... these can be great incentives to drink (deeply.)

Hooked Worms

A mysterious angst, to be sure. We cloak these situations and feelings in words that sometimes reveal a little; sometimes too much. The reader is wont to continue if only for the allure of empathy for the agonized mind.

Posing Poppies

I understand the sentiment but I also understand this.. that under the "right" circumstances anyone (and I do mean anyone) will react with violence/war. Sadly, it takes such little provocation and there are those that profit and delight from such provocations. For many, this is repugnant but it is like rebelling against gravity. Perhaps the solution to controlling both gravity and war will come when we least expect it. Let's hope the solution is tenable.

Tongues of Soft Cotton

Rhythmic circles of the night, hold moon-struck others firm and tight. "...whispering, 'Open wide!'"

Silly Salads

Estrangement by rearrangement... Not a trier so much... God loves gravity.

Bifurcated Adieus

I tell myself this all the time. Sometimes I listen and sometimes I don't. Of course that's the self-centered interpretation. The other seems a bit less caring.

Dainty Detentes

What is the difference between a lament and a bitch? Emotion. Different kinds of emotion. However this has both kinds as near as I can tell. One is more visceral, the other more melancholy. In my opinion you've done a fine job of stitching them both together into a jagged seam; it's gonna leave a scar. Sometimes those scars fade over time until you can hardly see them. Others, well they are kind of keloid and stand out like a brand. Some learn from their experiences and wear them as a badge of honor. Others try to cover them up and are embarrassed about them. I wonder which this will be?

Chapter 2

Purple Sticky Notes

This one caught my eye, XY. I really like it. Both for the content and your claim, "I don't understand what I have written." I don't either but I am compelled to apply a stream-of-consciousness review toward that end. If we rehearse in reverse then killing more requires additional living - a resurrection of the broken man of cindered stick that can give more but does not see - when the spoon bends then the mind is free. These stains of which you talk about become the art of outside-in when viewed in mirrored time and then... the windowed storm, framed and hung upon the wall is too an art; from heart it's sung. Stars, moon and sun whirl as Mayan rites seen unfurl - analogous razor flint, we dance on the edge of life and bleed - snaking blood over those fish hook bones drips on stones and shakes to earth in an attempt at perpetual finality.

Blank Minds Applaud

A deep and profound meditation. I'm happy that you were able to remember and share as much as you did; and with such compelling words and lyric phrasing.

Daubs of Dapper Dan

On this side of the pond in the 30's we had "Spanky and the Gang" (B&W movies). One of the characters, Alfalfa, - his mum always parted his hair down the middle but, as the fellow in your excellent piece above, he would (on occasion) rearrange the look to lessen the sissyfied comments from the gang. A nice poke from the way-back machine, XY. ☺

Sighing Sunbeams

Well, hey, you have to give o'le captcha credit. It did get the first part of xanthophyll. That would have been a little too spooky though, huh? ☺ Five pointy little leafy fingers representing one of the most prevalent attributes from life's genetic blueprint. I mean besides the fact that most mammals have five digits there's the possibility that this poem has (at least) five major philosophical propositions lurking beneath the poetic facade. Sorry, just my imagination acting up again. Incurable - so I've been told.

Drops of Crazy Glue

...and even the conifer sheds it's needles. It's just better at hiding them under her skirt. That poor old Scotch

Pine doesn't even have a kilt to lift anymore. Alas. But, I digress... what an excellent poem. It hums a little tune while dancing a graceful samba as it crosses the distance to that cookbook on the kitchen counter where it flips to find just the right recipe.

Chewy Nougat Centres

Wow! This poem sure spans the generations, XY! Some of those references are only ghosts of Christmas' past and the others seem to play leap-frog with the leap years. Thanks for opening the old photo albums in my head. There's a lot of good memories there. ☺

Inches of Rowdy Red Trousers

Machiavelli meets Nostradamus in the Berkshires awaiting Elvira, mistress of the late night photoreceptor burnout extravaganza. Oy! You do have a way with this stuff, X. Now, I must go and bang my head against the radiator - see if I can get a little more heat in this freezer. Bless those who wheeze and sneeze and cough for they shall suffer most before the lesser.

Light Shadows

Marvelous. Really. I/you/we... see - one of many possible manifestations of existence. This is not uncommon for those that have come here, to this place, prewired with the proper frequencies of mind, body and spirit. Although I can admire the visage it is even more intriguing for me to contemplate what will be done with this um, let's just call it "information", shall we? What should anyone do with these possibilities? Embrace? Reject? Select? Protect? We, the angels, both dark and light, select the paths we use for flight.

Best Friends (that are not death)

I am tempted to say something like, "Love it! Now you're seeing clearly. Everything you know and love is going to turn to sh*t and die." But I had another thought a while ago that this poem reminded me of... what if, just what if... the power of death is the illusion that it exists? If I were to believe this in any way, on any level then I might have "the faith that surpasses all understanding."

Geometric Coffee

Ah, XY... this one express an eccentricity that approaches the harmony of the sphere. It's almost 3-dimensional as it attempts to teach a sort of transcendence by virtue of circular observations. It compliments, nicely, morning's coffee contemplations.

Dreaming Expectations

It is either a student-mentor or, more likely, a child-parent vocalization that strives to find a compromise between the external forces of another's expectations versus those of the dreamer. It is written in an clear, honest voice and needs only a small amount of grammatical tweaking to make it worthy of a wider audience; should that be the goal. Either way, nicely done, XY.

Chapter 3

Becalmed Sailor'd Souls

Offerings of the flesh... yes, yes indeed. From that altar'd deckage - there the shore seems distant and the tremulous waves are a constant reminder of where, too often, we find ourselves drifting. This little "offering" has a lot of truth in it... potent, flavored with the same wisdom that becalmed sailors acquire as the rations become strained between mutual acquaintances. At those times the flesh demonstrates a mind of its own that exists in exile but is never far from that conscious morality that captains respective ships.

Toots of the Little Horn

Ah yes, the commutation with exacerbation; an all too familiar situation. I do like the manner of your exposition and commentary on this lamentable condition of contemporary travel, XY, my friend. Nicely phrased with aptly chosen verbiage.

PGFY's

Classic X! I'd know that style anywhere... you ready to beam up?

Screaming, Clacking Keyboard-damning Demons

Hey, XY! ☺ I find it most annoying when my efforts to comment are destroyed by the site editor. You'll just have to use your imagination. It was all about creativity and creative style - biblical versus derivative. I admonished you to contemplate both and to begin to review other peoples works; in order to help you become a better writer. (sniff, snoot) Then I wrote something arrogant and snotty and quippy - as a final zinger - I think that's when the gods decided they'd had enough and declared that my minuscule rant merited summary destruction. Sometimes the "Save Comment" is more like a "Banish This Crap Review To Hell" button.

Crumbly Dirt Cakes

You need to start shopping at a different store. One that has a different selection of goods and services. One that turns the ventilation on once in a while so you don't suffocate yourself and make your skin too blue so that you fall, hit your head, bleed blood-red on the snow and then have to go where they fix up such wrecks. I'll season this piece with a little tyme-time; maybe that will perk it up enough so that I don't get too dizzy reading an extra allocation of suffocation. That does it. You're on probation. No more negation just perspiration as you seek the intoxication that is a life well-lived. Go forth and snocker.

Bus Tokens and a New City Map

A crack is a void - a place where something was and is no longer. A crack that fills you is actually unfilling you - thus the blank map of selfness. But on the bright side, if you drown in comfortable despair then at least those cracks will be filled with something. Hola! ..let us greet the nothingness together.

Rolls of Clear Blue Ice-dice

Ohooo... like this one! Excellent metaphor and allusion for a soul that weighs the risk of love against the emptiness of its absence. A hopful and hesitant piece that shines with an innate innocence so often found in the young.

Broken Guitar Picks

I haven't quite decided if you like these emotions or not.
It seems like you want to forget them (in a way) but at
the same time you're enjoying the rage - like it brings a
certain purpose, fills an empty space on the shelf where
"stuff" use to be. So, he did a jones on you, a monkey
hopping jones and now you're going cold turkey with the
shakes; smashing crap and so on. Does the rage lessen the
sadness? An old movie (a lot of'em probably) say, "..don't
get mad - get even." and then there's the rest that preach
some sort of forgiveness - him, you, the world - be one with
the universe. So, what's to be done about this accident
of life? Anything? Probably not... "Ok folks, move along,
move along. Nothing to see here."

Spooky Little Paper Dolls (Eeek!)

Wow, this one ... readable, spooky, tragic. The reap-
ing and sowing message mixed with "sewing" by ??? paper
dolls??? That is one creepy vibration that you chose for
amplification; so, what in tarnation has gotten into you?
Wormed its way through the hay, on that day, while you
played.. my crow says to your crow, "Caw! Caw! Caw!"

Painter Eyes

I appreciate your eyes, XY. They take us places and
point out the fellowship of your mind with surroundings
of the moment. Paint on.

Burning Candles

You write what is in your heart - that can never be wrong (technically speaking, a maxim but it's mostly true). Sadly, in order to accomplish your stated goal this will need a wider audience. I suggest you start by doing readings... street corners, coffee shops, parks ... anywhere you can find an audience. Develop an activism strategy that empowers others to carry your message with a commitment to action. But beware.. do not collect one dime yourself. Research "the charities" that focus on your cause and then "suggest" actions that direct energies/resources in their direction. In this way you provide no venue for those who would be your enemy; and you will have enemies. Be well, do good work and keep writing, Bluef.

Thoughtful Trees

Yes, there seems always to be more to life than what we may perceive at any given moment in time. It is a worthy message for a poem. High quality work. Please continue your studies and poetry.

Chapter 4

Smiling Faces

"We miss you. You have not disappointed. We believe in you. Baby is.. come see for yourself. Come hold us in your warm embrace. We wait for you.", said the angels.

Snakes in a Basket (lift the lid at your own discretion)

I must label this.. it is curious, perhaps unique. There is the probabilistic reference - snakes, bones - "throw dem bones" - taking chances. It's almost like trying to read Tarot cards... read to divine the future, for reassurance ("..tell me – everything – is ok."). "..venom leaks into my brain" - the Cups - sometimes poisoned - Socrates death - a condemnation by society. "..a matter of finding prey" or by analogy finding "pray" (hoping for an outcome other than that envisioned.) Friends, wrapping themselves about one.. could be interpreted as supportive or smothering, suffocating ... choking the life away. All in all a very intriguing poem/write.

One-size Silhouettes

Hmm... somehow, this connected with me, XY, on a lot of different levels. I like the choices, the word-color and short brush strokes of phraseology. It's a simple (yet complex) message and it's easy to "see" it (the action) unfold. Plus, there's no particular human silhouette - it's a one-size-fits-all. In my opinion I think it's one of your best.

Encouraging Whispers

...and I miss you too. Remember when I once thought that a porch was an extravagance? An unwarranted labor during those summer months of unceasing toil. But you encouraged me to see the wisdom with your own particular vision regarding its utility. I shared your vision of the future then, as I do now; and it gives me some comfort to recall our old conversations. I won't encourage you to listen to my whispers again. I know it's hard. It's been a long time for you. But, take heart - you have lost nothing and we will soon be together again.

Tadadadada

Ah, this IS the swamp, isn't it? ..just know that everybody walks through this swamp. Many are eaten by the critters (after all, we're just food for something) but some do make it out the other side. What's on the other side of the swamp you say? Well, it could be a lot of things but mostly it's a multiple-choice quiz:

A.) The other side of the swamp. B.) The desert. C.) The

ocean. D.) The airport. E.) A film crew making the next-gen edition of Swamp Thing. F.) Pappy in a pirot with a bucket-o-gator-gizzards. G.) Happy The Clown (turn around, go back through the swamp - it's better, trust me.) H.) Angels (..sorry, you didn't make it but *BONUS* you're going to Heaven!) I.) A giant floating eyeball, telepathic, {What are you doing in my swamp young person-thing?} J.) A tree full of Blue Jays (an omen, for sure - go to store, buy fruit, you're hungry.) K.) A campfire circled with little kids and marshmallows on sticks. (move, slowly, to the right...) L.) Uncle Frodo's cabana-cabin (Fear grips you, hunger grips you, gator com'n - don't let IT grip you!) M.) Mmm.. why am I doing this? I don't know. Really, I don't. But that's enough choices for now. Make up some of your own. It's good for your sparkles. ☺

Chocolate Roses

On every continent there are beasts. Wild, ravenous yet soft as fleece and they lure us to untimely ends but we have keen senses and can sniff the wind. It smells of things musky, dark and damp that crawl and squirm and in the shadows prance. All these things we learn to fear yet they abhor true love and in that you may find some cheer and guidance as you travel on your way; be safe, play hard, learn lots and live to love another day.

Free Transformations

I getting the sense that you love to write about impossible conflict. It's a mental approach more than an emotional approach. Emotions are baggage to this sort of exposition but also a necessary set of props for any of the actual unexplainable inner turmoil to have any footing in the comprehensible. The real horror of it all is that it may (if not already) begin to mirror the other side of the water's surface. But the bubbles of fantasy also follow the same rules of nature and will shape themselves according to a conservation of sanity. There's no harm in dying. The harm is in not trying.

Black, Shiny, Poe(etic) Raven Feathers

i LIKE it .. deliciously gloomy, desolate and despondent — makes me want to imagine myself as some once-admired-and-now-forgotten piece of decomposing Fall Splendor. "..thorny vines dusted with virgin snow" .. gives me the thought to prick my finger and suck the life blood from myself to see if sustenance can be forced into a circular relationship. The writing is just awful good too. ☺

Birthday Trunks

Well, yes, happy birthday mom. For sure. But what's this bit about "the trunk?" I thought it was an elephant giving birth or something like that? Did I take it too literally? Sorry. ☺

Horizontal Pigtails

Is there some deep, dark hidden writer-thing in this? If there is then you need to come clean because I'm thinking miscarriage (of justice) or abortion (of thought) or worry (about nothing at all); all wrong, I'm sure. If you wore pigtails I'd be tempted to hold them out horizontal and say, "My, my ... you do write some doozies!"

Karma Kaptchas

Seriously, you've got this sex-crazed captcha working overtime on your karma train; it's insane! BTW, this one is excellent. 😬

Enigmatic Pluralities

This is very enigmatic. Although the message is singular the thoughts it instills are plural.

Words That End in Ess

I like it, I love, its great - don't hit me. Tiger, squirrel, lioness ... a perfect trio and makes me think of words that end in "ess." But, doing that would make me more of a mess so I'll confess it was perfectly prepared to pander to my peculiar predilection for pomposity. The lioness reminds me more of a wascaly-wabbit. The duck, the rabbit and I must now say, "goodbye!" The lioness hath her Pryde and the tiger nearly died. ...waiting for "Squirrel Heart" (the movie).

Unicorn Sunshine

I am not letting you near my portfolio - drive away all my securities, eh? Poverty should ensue methinks! However, the rest, no problem. I'm kinda happy now but glue the horn back on the unicorn and we're good till sunshine shows itself again. ☺

Resplendent Trains

"chugga-chugga-chugga" .. yes but that was before my time and yours I suspect. Nice how it reminded not of a train but of hot chocolate (or worse). Still, this is very colorful and personal and exudes a certain wonderful resplendent charm. I like it. ☺

Whimsy Randoms

Reads like a couple of throws of the i-ching ("Yì Jīng"). The way that the similes are used seem somewhat at odds with the apparent intent and/or message. They require grounding that is unavailable for most readers I suspect. But, it's just a thought. The words themselves have an likable constructive position throughout so there is none of the frailty of pure whimsy.

Chapter 5

Godzilla Tsunami

A ton of people... average adult weight, 175 pounds. 2000 pounds per ton.. so that's like 11.42 people being swallowed by the sea, right? Is that just once or per unit time? Perhaps like 11.42 people per second.. yea, that would be a lot - a tsunami - perhaps from a meteor impact or an avalanche off the coast of a distant land mass. Wow! Like a hybrid cross between Godzilla and Mothra!

On a lighter note, I like the reference to something lower than hell. That's something to think about. I mean hell is supposed to be the ultimate darkness, right? Now you tell me there's something even worse. Yikes! I'm not gonna ask where YOU go on vacation.

Liked it.. you control the dark like a walk in the park with a dog and a bark and a lark .. i snark, "Snark! Snark!" Come on do it with me.. "Snark! Snark! Snark!" Feels good doesn't it? Anything that makes YOU feel good makes bad things feel terrible. They just cringe, shrivel up and go away. Ayup, they do.

Smile with me... ☺

Ugly Humans

You first mistake was in thinking you are human. You
are not. Human is just a word. You are more than a word.
When you are born, the convention is to give you a designation, so you will know when energies are being directed at
you. But, you don't need that designation to know when
energies are being directed at you. You sense them with
a multitude of facilities; some you don't even know you
possess (yet.) There are some fundamental truths that you
either already know or suspect. Permit me to share some.

1.) Everything that lives dies. [..guessing you already
knew this one.]

2.) Every day you live something else MUST die. [The
law of universal balance is immutable.]

3.) There are both external and internal forces and you
may direct some of each.

4.) How you choose to employ the forces under your
control determines your "destiny."

5.) Emoting here is almost the equivalent of putting a
bucket over your head and talking to yourself; hardly anyone is listening and even fewer probably care. But.. by the
laws of probability - some do. Good luck finding them if
that is one of the choices you choose to invoke.

6.) Good and bad are words - just like love, hate, pride,
ignorance, greed, lust, envy ... all of the seven deadly sins
and more. But you (and those around you) actually give

them "meaning." They have no meaning until your experience assigns a collective of personal memories to them.

7.) You write as a means to understand the environment, realm, world, ... that you find yourself within/without/in-doubt/ready-to-shout-and-pout ... but it's safe, isn't it? Until you put those words out where others can get at them, pluck them from your carefully tended trees-of-knowledge, vines-of-experience, flowers-of-indescribable-beauty. Then it's war. It's dog-eat-dog, it's cats and dogs sleeping together its everything you've been led to believe .. until you experience it for yourself and extrapolate a difference.

8.) Then there's "truth" and "lies." A multitude of sins/grins/kicking-of-shins goes with each incarnation, each infatuation, each elation of ego manipulation; yours, theirs. Thankfully the non-humans don't know or care, right? They bite because they're hungry or afraid - rarely because they're angry or mean. Of course some are just sick - wired that way from birth. Are you sick? I don't think so. I hope..

Light Battles

So, the thought is that if we turn to light and truth and love then the battle is done. Still have to fight the battle but it's already won. Good, light and love triumph over evil and darkness. Hold that thought... that's the key, isn't it? Got it. What's my reader score? :)

Circular Grumpy Grumps

Um.. a grumpy old man being grumpy about being a Grumpy Old Man?

Lonely Walls

That's the way it happens sometimes, isn't it? Experience grief.. build walls - to keep safe. But then forever alone.. so alone. Good one, XX.

Unsettling Ambiguities

Unsettling.. mostly because of the ambiguity in this phrase, "knowledge that you loved." Was it the love of knowledge or the knowledge of love? That one may love and therein find some solace is speculative at best. This is not, for some, quid pro quo or quod est demonstratum.

Thinking Stones

This seems to support, in its own curious way, something I am wont to say .. on any given day .. that not everything that bounces between our ears is fit to publish. I like a little on toast as jam because then I don't feel so foolish when I get into one. Amen.

Wanting Because

Wow! .. much too solvent to be mixed with such shades of bright, middling spectral tones. This is certainly not your usual palette, X. What on earth am I to do? Confused, alone, a dismal day but these words; like birds that wing their way through those cloud studded skies. I lie and cry... goodbye, goodbye.

Running Fans

I have the sudden urge to offer you one of my babble pills. I take these on such occasions as you mention up above, when the stars twinkle and I feel the loss of love. The silly things they make me say seem to take all my cares away and I am left to laugh and snort and ask for buttons named "ABORT." It goes without saying I am not a prude and that I resist being rude for if every a one I knew that tore my heart up from the goo I would say her name was X... you. Goonasnockers, Miffyall! ☺

Tepid Asterisks

I was immediately drawn to the end words of each line. I had the urge to put them at the front and take every third word and throw it on the end. Why? Why? Why? Is nothing sacred? It seems I am compelled to pick up the fight for black and white. But no I shall resist and instead I shall live out the remainder of my tepid life as an asterisk. A symbol of something never appropriate to be seen in the company of civilized words. Adieu my X. Adieu. Oh, by the way, 100 for you. (Just because I can.)

Alien Slippers

Ack! Not every alien abduction is "tainted" but if you put your slippers by the bed when you go to sleep and then wake up the next morning with flip-flops - well, that would be a serious contradiction in the terms of endearment. My dear, what has gotten in to you? ☺

Carefree Commutes

Well, this is different. I like it - a lot. I guess the note that resonated the most was the memories of driving along the PCH; Santa Monica, Long Beach, RPV and all points 50 miles north and south of LA. Of course those days of carefree madness are long gone but as with yours - not forgotten. Nicely done, **XX**. Nicely done.

Chapter 6

Love Handles

Without doubt, there are some things that are hard to say and still harder to come to terms with. In this I read not so much of human lust or vanity but coming to terms with the arc-of-life and all that implies. That you have chosen feminine beauty as the handle on this well-wrought cup - one from which we may grasp, lift and take a sip; this quality of the brew is excellent - smokey with memory and just a hint of bitterness. It is the kind of thing that goes well with the reality that morning will eventually turn into evening as our sun sets. I applaud this vignette of life, this expose of that distant corner of human existence where the story is not just words but someone's reality - well told and well written. Thank you, XX.

Cracking Shells

A very good poem, XX. Now, for some of my usual non-sense... The cause of those mislaid words? I think there's (possibly) an alien mind-dampening field surrounding the planet. It is keeping "sensitive" people from sensing and experiencing with their usual acumen. It's probably a prelude to some form of invasion. Perhaps they'll turn it off soon - so we can experience the full effect of their Shock-&-Awe campaign. The poets will be the first to be thrown "...inside the killing jar"; easy pickings too. They'll see them in the dark. Self-illuminated from the glow - ooze from those mind "...cracks, fractures like an eggshell releasing the sun."

Civil Emotions

I think the last thing you want is for me to assume the persona and get inside the head of supposed-to-be for a pithy comeback. Let's just say I "felt" this one but not in the way you might imagine. I'd call this write - provocative. That's it.. I felt provoked. But, fortunately, my sense of civility was stronger than the emotions seething up inside me. Excellent pot stirring, XX.

Scenic Train Rides

Yes, XY, this is a different train. The scenery is stunning though and I've yet to make up my mind on the nature of the power source that pulls this elegant coach toward a cheering throng at the station platform. It choos and I chew.. "Waiter, another cup, if you please." ☺

Deleted Writings

A gripping story from start to.. oh, it's not finished is it? You're not going to leave us hanging here like this are you? You've got the ideas, that's for sure. My main observation, and it's only an observation, is that the main character is "talking" to us (the readers.) You might wish to try and "show" the story in a less journalistic style. Of course there are the minor typos, omissions and grammar thingies but I'm sure you already knew that. Oh, and thanks for putting up more than one chapter. So many will just dribble it along with a chapter a day - that gets very tiresome and it's then so easy to lose interest in the story. Thanks again and I hope to read another chunk (or the finale) soon! Nice job, X! ☺

Eraser Case

This is why I always carry an eraser with me when I meet new people. If it doesn't work out between us then I write it in a journal and then erase it. My mind.. the journal.. tomorrow is a new day. Thanks for reminding me, X.

Cobalt Doors

The mind works in mysterious ways... and there is certainly a mystery here. Delicately painted shades, the words our thoughts invade and open a cobalt door. An auto-erotic moment stretched to infinity with the delicate pull of irresistible imagination.

[X, awarded the Prussian Blue Crossing My Mind medal for Valorous Fantasy.]

Quality Thoughts

The reader has awakened. The reader has contributed to the message. Who/what is the author?

Metaphorical Hats

It is said that every journey begins with a single step. In this case a not-step. Herein lies the lesson. As you and other poets (myself included) have pointed out, mostly to each other, the message is different for each reader. I would extend that to include each writer. Oh, by the way, it really is a good poem in my opinion too. Feel free to curtsy as I perform a deep bow and flourish of the metaphorical hat. ☺

Smiling Hooks

Oh, here's the hook, "...How is my reflection smiling when my flesh isn't?" Now, you've got us wanting more! But, before you do please tell me this is nothing you EVER want to offer to a serious publisher (for money, fame, fortune, etc.).

Past Sins

I am hard put to know where to begin with this one. You've pulled out some wonderful and dark magyk from that place where few dare tread. Every line a slash of the sword, every stanza the crash of the battle axe upon our shields of civility, of what we thought the world was before being felled senseless by the blow. As we lay, bleeding, gasping for some respite in this battle of the gods there is the terminus of something similar to the priest's confessional. A place where secrets are revealed in the here and now; perhaps to seek atonement for sins of the past. ...an enormously powerful piece to occupy such a small space. I should not wonder if the page explodes, turns dark and runs shrieking from itself.

Chapter 7

Mystery Menus

I wonder if this is a gender-specific fantasy myth - meeting the mysterious woman in some social setting and exchanging something of life for wisdom? It has all the elements of a good myth, a good story. The sketch is rough but it holds promise. Perhaps you will develop the painting in time to come?

Respectful Fish

It is a startlingly good poem, XX. A Möbius strip of thought/emotion that is, in the end, forever twisted and circular. I note the past tense at the end and presume neither survived the ordeal; well perhaps the writer. One cannot know these things for certain, can we? However, I will request vegetarian for any wake, out of respect for the fish.

Thumb Twiddles

Heh, yes, permutations can be fun. ☺ This is not only written backwards but right-to-left; rather Japanese and hieroglyphic in its freedom - more of scriber's art than message if you know what I mean. Language, "..born like all, pure and innocent." Ayup. ☻

Wondering Children

It is a time of wonder and learning, isn't it? Childhood... and you take us back there so well with this. Delightful, X. Thank you.

Attracting Primeval

This is primeval, really. Can you see Ogette admiring the way that Ogg swings his club as he cracks the skull of some opposing clansman bent upon expanding territory? Those basic attributes of strength, courage, the rage and swagger of success - those things that will keep meat on the fire and predators from the cave. How could she not be attracted to him? That you've managed a contemporary translation makes it all the more admirable and one that we may relate to on a visceral level.

Eloquent Senses

Ah, XX... love, as experienced through the senses; surely as varied as the combinations and levels that may be experienced - in this case by the allegory of taste. I think you're right too, that there are flavors yet to know but your life is not over so.. let the grand experiment continue. It occurs to me that it really isn't the words that fail so much as we, the readers, through our lack of similar experience. Time and circumstance, the enemy of knowing, experiencing those gradients of love. Without the knowing, without a reference point of comparison, we will always be lost, unmoved by even the most eloquent and deftly chosen phrase. The fault is not yours... it's ours; we just need to get out more.

Soaking Moonbeams

I wonder what you might write about, later, if many of your ardent fans here should suddenly show up on your doorstep some evening; while that water is boiling and the pasta is swimming in those salted eruptions? Of course it's a fantasy but an interesting one I think. What would your face look like upon opening the door? Wide-eyed, innocent, unsuspecting or crazed with fear that the community collective had come to assess the adherence to some unwritten standards of hospitality? How would you remember the evening that wore on - possibly late into a dew-soaked moonlit morning? How would our dear XX capture that scene? How might she immortalize the moment and those who yearn to toast greatness and in so doing become a part of history?

Melancholy Throats

Ah, yes, it can seem like that at times; melancholy I
mean. The odd thing here is that you've befriended it.
Rather like Robin Williams' portrayal of the depressive
atmosphere of pre-glasnost Russia (Moscow on the Hud-
son). I suppose it manifests differently for everyone - that
you describe it here as a falling into darkness as something
wraps about the throat; that's rather different. I wouldn't
have imagined that as an artifact of melancholy. I've always experienced it as a lingering blues or subtle depression (perhaps erroneously). Ah well, best leave the details
to the professional, eh? In the end, a nice rendition, XX.

Babbling Brooks

It's depressing, really... isn't it? But, consider the brook
that babbles to itself, hidden in the woods (lovely, dark
and deep). Can a poet give it life, a witty voice and a
measure of self-assurance such that it continues onward
with the assistance of carefully chosen words, time and
gravity? ...perhaps toward a more (seemingly) purposeful
end? Never think your bounty goes unnoticed. Kiss me,
quick.. I have bees to place.

Curious Cares

It happens more than one might care to think about it. The mountain assimilates them... do you wonder when they appear later? Sometimes much later. Say it... write it... do it to keep from screaming or just because your curious if you're still sane; sometimes it helps - sometimes it doesn't. We were all curious... once.

Balcony Applause

A wolf will gnaw its own leg off to get out of a steel trap... I've seen people write like this and it's usually because the left half of their brain is trying to devour the right half (or vice verse). However, it is redeeming in that it provides a focal point for contemplation while zit-picking in the mirror of life. For that you get echoey applause from the balcony.

Chapter 8

Tattered Hats

An excellent Andy-Warhol-like mind painting ... soup can brain purge; but you left the label on so no discount for you. Otherwise, a gay piece that exudes a most cheerful anger in a colorful sort of way. I'm thinking your chest was much relieved of the forces of inertialess gravity mass matters... mad as a tattered hatter.

Melding Minds

Interesting. A gross interpretation of a relevant concept with psycho-sexual sublimation of trans-local perception. To put it bluntly, it seems your mind has been "melded."

Notable Quotes

"No, I have never experienced writer's block, although I sometimes have to wait a long time before I receive inspiration for the next book." ~ P. D. James (Phyllis Dorothy James White, London, England)

Mooze Benders

Garp snarvel! Usses meesus be splatzn vwerds alumen da dark un skaireez. Wotchu sez mooze bender?

Sneezing Poets

Yes, XX... and this is what happens when poets sneeze. Kachoofish! Kaselfish! Ashparkle! Aww, relish! ...now where did that mustard go? I'm glad you lightened up a bit. I thought I was going to have to grab another box of tissue from the captain's chest.

Ragged Lines

Poignant and sad, so very sad. The actions that we are compelled to take; compelled by forces beyond our comprehension. Such understanding is at times implicitly understood and at the same time beyond reckoning. You cut a ragged line, XX.

Changing Matters

Here! Here! ... a call to action if ever there was one. May your words find for you the power you seek and in turn it change those things that to you matter. Bon, tre bon.

Guilty Victims

A tragic poem; so sad... yes victims, they especially, but we are all victims and all guilty in some way or another. If only words could stir to action those courageous imped-iments that are sorely needed. It must weigh upon you - that you make this your first offering here.

Struggling Decisions

Nice story, X. Now, I encourage you to write the follow up story. Personally, I would like to see the protagonist struggle with feelings of accomplishment, altruism, fatal-ism, ego, and the ultimate blow; the system only "seemed" to work (at first) because there was something missing - something secret that he finally discovers only to realize that the world isn't ready for it. What does he do at that point? Who/what is hot on his tail to make sure he doesn't get the chance to make that decision? Is art imitating life or the opposite?

Warrior Queens

I'm going to make a couple of comments. Some will, I think, show how much you've improved since this was

written and the other; well, it's just plain silly. Let's go
with the silly first.

SILLINESS

I read the first stanza and do you know what popped into
my head? Paul McCartney singing "Silly Love Songs" but
with the lyrics changed to "...sticky wittle wove swongs"
aka Elmer Fudd. Don't ask me why.

D'Arcy Wentwork Thomas ~ ON GROWTH AND
FORM (a famous book, find a copy and read it - you'll
like it)

You no longer burden your poetry with the sense that
it must needs be dressed in proper attire to attend the
Grand Ball. That's a relief; really. However, there is the
saving grace of the close-coupled in-line rhymes that distract from the blatant formalism and give it a more natural
flow. And yet, after a few more stanzas, I see that even it
was dressed to kill, rather like a cymbal going off in the
middle of Sunday Prayers. Although I must admit to being
startled by the gong, I still had a revelation and saw the
portal of the deities and altar that accepted this youthful offering. There is no denying the lust of its desire to
exist; somewhere where it will be accepted and loved and
cherished. That much is most sincere but it lies between
the lines, hidden deep within the psyche of the inspiration
that drew it from a dark slumber.

I leave you with a sweet embrace and thought to sink
my fangs into your throbbing neck when next we meet my
dark warrior Queen.

Chapter 9

Big Dismal Boo Boos

This sounds like you're about ready to move in to the old motel down the street. The one with the flickering neon sign and the vending machine that only works part of the time. The one with the seedy desk clerk in the T-shirt with gravy stains on it who continues to watch the TV in the back room as you bang the hell out of the bell on the counter. One good thing though... the rent's as cheap as the bedding and furniture imply it should be. Some tips though: don't trust "housekeeping" (keep your good stuff with you - always), don't accept rooms next to the pool (earthquake water tsunami), always check under the bed and in the closet and never, never leave food crumbs on the night stand overnight; the roaches are... huge. Oh, nice poem BTW. ☺

.

Emotional Batteries

An exquisite weaving of loneliness and depression and that grand voyage on a rudderless ship. They, the quintessential "they", must give out free tickets on that special ship. I see no other explanation for the random, sun bleached bones on an otherwise pristine beach. This piece, it glistens in a bright light that casts stark shadows from those jutting outcrops, just there above the heart shaped rock below the lighthouse that beckons the foolish ones upon these shoals of the soul. You should consider another motif because I have spent myself upon this one entirely. Something more uplifting next time if you please - I need a little help with the recharge of my emotional batteries.

Obscure Deaths

Why, oh why do the really good poems here just seem to wither and die in obscurity? Can it be that there are just so many of them that they simply get lost in this vast sea of words, this outpouring of human emotion cum-lingua-franca? Is this voice crying out in desperation not big enough or loud enough to be heard in the vastness of the universe? There's no cloud word for REALLY-GOOD-POEM. Perhaps that's it... or perhaps the tenants just abhor the whimpering of these new born things, eyes barely open, seeking the succor of attention from something larger than themselves; or someone that cares enough to read and scribble a few well-chosen thoughts in regard to their lyric stories.

As you imagined... one that cares, offering that hand,

dragging you up and then brushing your teary cheek with the back of that hand. It's real. You just have to believe it. It's been a while since you wrote this so I'll imagine that all is well and think happy thoughts of you in the present.

Bruised Petals

Damn... you seem to have exposed a part of my soft underbelly. In reflection, perhaps the flask was only a sort of false courage; for the cowardice - what man would not tremble in the presence of the goddess? The scraping of harsh, rusty iron upon virgin marble is less forgivable but none the less a pathetic attempt to construct a more enduring form of acrostic for what the eyes of man can never, ever fully see. But, it is the bountiful and cruel insensitivity that presupposes life must always have a goal and only the "ripest fruit" is worthy of such endeavor... a confirmation of that base nature as all possess. I am wont to gather up those bruised petals and embrace them as tenderly as is possible for they are the essence of life's glory; so beautiful, so fragile, so fleeting. For me, you've done well with this one, XX.

Egoless Moons

I confess, I date everything too... perhaps it's my inner ego, the little one tucked inside the big one, it has this curious fantasy that someday it will be famous (or perhaps infamous) and it delights in fantasizing the conversations of future biographers, "Oh, that was so helpful - to have dated everything. Now we may construct an accurate and orderly time line of the rise-to-fame and untimely demise." I suspect the moon influences the inner ego while the sun the outer, larger one. You may consider me one of the throng of telescopic stalkers that revel in those "powder blue mornings" while observing "dandruff flakes shaken off the shoulders of the sun." Please, permit me to bump your upliftiness another notch in the positive direction as I reread this piece and admire a coming-of-age, a maturation of growth in thought and style that, having regrouped, seems determined "not to be outdone or outshone."

Noticing Universes

This makes me wonder if anyone was watching when the first, the very first phoenix arose from the ashes. It makes me assume that mythic creature's composure as it surveys the circle of ash within which it stands, reeling from the memories of lives past and revelation of freedom and rebirth. I shudder as I contemplate the pain of the past and the possibilities of the future. I breath, no longer forlorn... I am reborn.

An inspiring write, XX. Take heart, the universe notices your endeavors.

Hellish Essense

Sadly, I think this may be the essence of hell, such as it may be imagined; to become aware of the suffering that we may have caused, that others may have endured on our behalf... and knowing that we cannot help them now. Let there be light.

Dark Soup

Honestly, how would Poe react to this reading? Imaginatively, I think he'd do his best to instill in you that which you fear in jest. "Come, lad, sit in that chair beside my hearth's open grate and let us speak of that upon which you've prate." "How is it that you've come to be within my my house, my mind; to see perhaps my wizened soul... or merely sip my dark soup from your porcelain bowl?" ... to be continued.

Raven Cloaks

Perhaps you believe you have entered your "gallery" stage of life? One where all of the inspiration and the master works have been rendered complete from body and soul... standing or hanging, illuminated under focused spots as weekend spectators, wine glass in hand, discuss the merits of light and shadow? I beg to differ, if so. These lines, these colors cum emotion are merely the dormant seed of greatness-in-waiting... they are but the foundation layers of those cantilevered escapades calling the brave, foolhardy writer to pirouette out to dangers edge and pen life, brilliantly, upon a reader's waiting mind. Those WAR pipes call you still, I think. They only need someone (some thing) to breath new life into the drones... hear them? Hear the distant wailing of wind and reed... it yearns to call forth the magic of your imagination with its song. You should answer its call; oh moody, raven-cloaked warrior woman.

Rescue Duties

Terry Bird and you swimming in an ocean of tears... life, the guard-on-duty, comes to the rescue but there are ouchies to mend and gritty sand to wash away; it could take years. Nicely done... very nicely done.

ERRATA: "Well smile ..." ~ "We'll smile ..."

Q: Is honesty always the best policy?

New Flowers

Well, this is a strange one. Womb, crayons, kinder-art... and what is the "healthy omen" you speak of? Most perplexing this one. A new flower in the garden blooms.

Jailer Keys

No harm, no harm... and yet my arm hangs limp from my shoulder and it wasn't the plastic or the crystal. For any judgmental words, like wickedness, have only the meaning we give them when there are no better words for the unspeakable - the deviations from an equator with no correlation to temperature and position. The heat means no harm but kills just the same. Escape implies imprisonment but every mind is it's own best, most sturdily constructed prison. Selfless ego, the jailer that is the prisoner that holds the keys. Why are you still here?!

Chapter 10

Reckoning Dust

The winds are blowing, constantly now, since the birth of this planet and only it's death will still them. Dust... often choking, causing a shortness of breath but some can be watered and life will grow there. Like here. You are a force to be reckoned with, XY.

Axing Lambs

This seems an allegorical piece; a journey undertaken through the metaphor of forest - where forest seems to be people... a surround of trees that do not know if they are oak or willow or a soft white cottonwood planted by the random winds. It speaks of gender finding itself ("...and I wake up on a lamb-coat of no shame") and of an acceptance of things; perhaps without conditions. There are references to places past - no longer as relevant but not forgotten; maybe never forgotten for that would be a violation of a sacred trust, wouldn't it? What's the ax for? The ax is for emergency use only, right?

Surface Tensions

Life as a metamorphosing water larva? No, no... must the soul, skimming the surface tension of life. A few well-gauged, energetic bursts and then transformation. But to what... to what?

Sincere Sarcasm

Have I ever mentioned that I love a good lamentation? They often reek of such delicately seasoned, righteous self-pity; and this seems no exception. A wonderful repast to serve those guests that would bring only a bottle of wine and a cheerful smile to court and woo the damsel locked away in her tower. No Rapunzel here... move along, nothing to see, just smoking timbers from the last barbaric horde that deigned to storm these gates. Little work had they to do for we flung them wide open knowing full well the plague would get them too... eventually. In the end they walked away counting coup but no real bravery was involved. A wonderfully written piece... and I give you a choice of entertainment. What shall it be? Sincerity or sarcasm? Choose now.

Returning Rabbits

You know that you've done something right when the rabbits come back, of their own accord, to nibble in your garden. ☺

Cool Droughts

Your works always seem to leave me with more questions than answers, Leslie. This one is no exception. You throw the poor reader one dried crumb... "written on a hot day." Is the reader the burnt map of Summer, a companion, a lover, a reflection of self? See what I mean? Nothing but questions. The mind labors and reeks with that stale-wind sweat. It drips but in my case, moistens a smile for I believe that distant rain is approaching. Cool and refreshing... soon to turn the dust of drought into a poultice to those who walk away over brown Spanish grass. No matter if real or imaginary - it is an excellent piece.

Willow Arms

Now, this is one of the you-that-are-we-cum-they I am hoping to read more of. I have to marvel at it all, really. I think sometimes, perhaps, you don't even realize you've done anything special until after the fact; am I right? But, you do have a nail, old and rusty, something sticking out of that repurposed lumber from another edifice... it snagged me, just here: "...the risen dead, would force my ghosts..." and it drew a drop of blood. It caused me to stumble slightly and I dropped my toy on the landing. Forced me to

stoop down and revisit that final step it did. I paused, reading again several times, to watch that pendulum swing...
the hypnotic flow of mind-time that seeps from that well
spring just above those willow arms. Arms that extend ever
outward, trying to embrace the all... always wanting more.

Worthy Compliments

I think there is more to this poem then meets the eye.
Somewhere there are "things" tucked away in your memories... things that want to be like this little mouse and
come out of his hole. Perhaps to see the world or have a
great adventure or perhaps to escape from one. Either way,
it is a very interesting narrative. There are a lot of curious connectives and the patterns are strange but alluring.
Certainly something worthy of compliment.

Imprisoned Seas

Is it the bane of later years that one should continually
question their worthiness for love? There are images that
allude to those wearing iron masks... imprisoned on islands
(of self) with only a single window (of soul) looking out
upon the sea (of their life). Such musings, such longings
must, of necessity, be required to endure until the time
when all things are resolved. The word poignant works
quite nicely with this one, XY.

Enduring Notions

Excellent, XX. These are thoughts that should be taken to heart by all. They speak of an honesty born of introspection that employs the fairly balanced scales of passion and selfless ego. This also speaks to the kind of friendship one might wish to strive for... let's encourage this notion to endure - if only for the moment.

Framing Pleas

There is an impression, a sense if you will, of a vague recognition that there is more than one form/kind of love. The supplicant here seems entrapped by one and is seeking release, to be free of the lesser form, so that they might experience a higher form (of love). The lines... sometimes they stutter just like the mind does when it is caught in a whirlwind of confusion and indecision but they seem to enhance the mood. The imagery signal brightness as the central theme and provides excellent framing of the final plea for a hopeful and happy outcome. Nicely written, XX

Chapter 11

Potted Plants

XY, I consider this one of your most coherent constructions to date. The reader's notes, while adequate, do not
provide insight into the inspiration and that is a void that
stands in stark contrast to this pleasing edifice. Rather like
a weed-strewn lot with plots for tenting standing beside a
well-kept Victorian B&B. However, it does little to detract
from the ingenious counterpoint of historical insight and
personal commentary on these complimentary societies so
compelled by their origins that they may appear to some as
a form of root-bound potted plant. I encourage you, whole
wholeheartedly, to pursue similar journeys with such vision
and alacrity.

Looming Torrents

When this child comes to know them so well that fear is a muted color of reality - what then?

... Fact or fantasy? What can I bribe you with that will encourage more reader notes?

I thought to myself, "I will commission Ms. XX for freshness in this wilting summer doldrums but then thought better of it as the promise of change and vast torrents loomed in the approaching weather."

Pondering Swallows

Love the formatting... a self-flagellation of sorts or perhaps a Rorschach test. I see a swallow-tail pondering Capistrano in the months ahead.

Promised Lands

It seems I caught you in mid-revision... oh well. I thought it was clever to see only a little punctuation that differentiated the titles but "; Version 2" works as well if but a bit more ho-hum.

The attempt at some bit of cheerful optimism is admirable as a continuation of bilateral reflectionism. (Don't worry, you won't find that in the dictionary but hopefully it does make some sort of sense.) It has to do with the penchant for the human mind to think in terms of the brain/body bilateral symmetry and an obtuse extrapolation of Darwinism (much like your 'borrowed' title).

However, in launching this fleet of hopeful voyagers we

note that they immediately run aground at the mouth of the sandy harbor shoals because of the moon and tides. The words: love, look, give, alone ... these all are minstrels of the heart, shanghaied as sailors on this life-wind tossed fleet. Such magnificent destinies have been charted and but few return, richly laden, from their long and tiresome journeys.

Such small words, to charm a nation... an yet they do so while merrily skipping, hand in hand, toward some gentile and verdant promised land.

Deleted Writings II

I very much like how you started here, in this first poem (reading bottom to top in your publishing timeline), with an acceptance of the dark things that can happen in life. It has a comfortable and orderly flow that most everyone finds "normal."

This is then the dark side of a contemplation of "Survival of the Fittest." Darwin would have no objection to these observations; nor do I. Every word is true in one respect or another. Only the angle of observation changes and it is infinitely variable.

I applaud the simplicity of your statements; the economy of well-chosen words that convey a precision of thought that implies either epiphany or excruciating meditations; possibly both.

[This review continues in the next... "]

A moment of substance in the furnace of life; the bronze is cast and she stands in the gallery of heroes - immortalized, blessed by a pantheon of gods and honored by supplicants in desperate need of a vision greater than themselves.

Tracing Brows

Wow... just wow. It reads like a long, woven cord of something... silk perhaps. But I'm blind and I can't see the colors... only feel the texture of the various types of threads that have been spliced together and knotted and woven into this amulet or bracelet - something like that. Then someone/something turns the lights on and there it is but totally different than what I'd imagined. Makes me want to traces some brow ridges with my fingertips.

Green Glass Bottles

An intriguing set of comments. It seems an amalgam of experiences that vex and perplex and demand some form of resolution/solution ... if that is even possible. Emotionally, it is gripping ... a sort of dark goo that permeates the consciousness as you read along; rather like that go-to in the park... the Wizard of Oz where Tin Man is the Terminator and Toto is the smartest one of the bunch and the currency of the realm is Oue'd-small-children in tiny transparent green glass bottles. Somewhere in there is a character much like Alladin's nemesis, calling out, "Hovercrafts for brooms..."

Apologetic Continuations

I see I didn't read far enough... this one is beautiful. "I hold these ideas paramount for I need and deserve something to love and someone who will love me or at least give it a try." ...and it is so. I'm glad you told me more about yourself. I think I must have scanned just the one, at random, and assumed all the others were the same. My mistake. They were not. It's a human foible thought isn't it? ...not looking any farther than the surface or the first thing we run in to; assuming that because the soup was unappetizing then the rest of the meal would be as well. Ah, well, continue to live... continue to learn. My apologies.

Noodle Buckets

I've heard it said that wolves mate for life. So this could be about the difference between a wolf and a dog. I wonder if you would write it that way? I bet it would be much harder without all of the TV and movie vignettes available for readers to call up in their minds as they read it. BTW, great poem oh friendly bucket of noodles. Gah! ...thinking of take-out. :)

Different Tastes

OK, count me with the bunch that see the anthropomorphic side of this piece. You need to come clean and give us the background of what was going through your mind when you wrote this. Honestly, I'm delighted that YOU are delighted that each reader has their own interpretation. That is certainly one of the great joys of writing in my opinion. We serve the same soup to all but it tastes different to everyone. Glorious! ... just like this little gem. ☺

Polite Kisses

It is polite to kiss the butterfly goodbye.

Chapter 12

Sparkling Strings

I feel like that intrepid explorer that braves the wilds of the jungle or in this case, the dusty nooks of a Writers' cafe... and I have found treasure! Oh, my brave and fearless writer! With such a string of precious, delicious, wonderfully sparkling string of innocent imaginings. "i wish for many things that cannot be. because miles are between us and because you do not wish for those things with me..." No, quite right. Sherlock is ever-busy but John is a good man and perhaps you will meet him still; him or someone like him. My compliments to the little chef inside your head. ☺

Brainiac Bric-a-brac

Well, now that I know you keep such horrid hours...
perhaps you won't mind if my little ship comes hovering
just outside your open window; just to say, "Hello!" and
wish you pleasant dreams? What rhymes with insomniac?
Brainiac... Brick-a-brac... ☺

Samarkand Thistle

tick tock whistle blows drip drop we know, it shows

Komodious P.

Something happens. I stare at Will. He stares back. I
get a chill.

Kow Finigan - Moo Fow

Fisher, Kasparov have nothing on you Fisher, Kasparov
adieu adieu Fisher, Kasparov in lieu in lieu Fisher, Kasparov et tu au bleu.

Ancient Drinks

Indulge me a moment... writers, this type of writing -
must of necessity invoke that portion of the mind that
synthesizes from things seen and learned using their imagination. However, for some, there is (always) the possibility,
fanciful perhaps but intriguing to contemplate, that they
draw from other lives. In your case, you seem "drawn" to

certain words, times... perhaps past lives? So, you are either currently taking a course in ancient Greek history or Mediterranean Cultures or you're just naturally "drawn" to these things. Which is it? What is the name of that water from which you drink?

Eclipsing Apples

What a beautiful answer to my previous question! I was a bit miffed that you didn't respond for a while but perhaps, if I may imagine, this could be that answer; of a sorts. I'll take it as such unless you would improve upon my sense of knowing. Perhaps we'll meet again - somewhere among the dust... just before you coalesce into one of those golden apples. Do you suppose there will be gnosis in that moment?

Love the finale...

" I write poetry in the diminishing eclipse of an Eden that no longer exists."

Construction Costs

A moth envying a butterfly... leaves me with a wistful, pensive moodiness. I long to say something cold and sobering to this moth about pretentious fluttering but feel that it would be wasted effort as the lesson has already been learned. An effective piece no matter the cost of construction.

Tolling Systems

"...and I am unafraid of the beyond, for all spirits leave the shell and hurtle toward the stars" Ah, but the knowing and the doing invoke an oft not-too-subtle difference. Here's to "pseudo-safety of the Above." BTW, those blemishes are intentional stamps of the here-and-now passport. The ferryman has updated the tolling system you know. ☺

Gnawed Slippers

Now, now... no need to get all ponderous and gloomy. It is a sort of life so enjoy it. Something else will come along sooner or later. Have a spot of something and enjoy my incessant chirping. I suppose I could find something willing to gnaw at your slippers on the way to the dustcart... bet that would get your attention, huh? ☺

Composting Sprouts

Uh, "ramiparous" ... not appealing to the haggard masses, yearning for poetry anymore, huh? ☺ I take it you've been doing a bit of gardening (or such)? If not, maybe you should. This thing is a mouth full and a mind full. I'm going to let it compost for a while... see what sprouts.

Chapter 13

Unique Pricks

Whoa! That is a most perplexing ending! A wonderful poem but just so complex and befuddling (to me). Is this the way it is, was, or will be? It pricks at the edges of my sensibilities in a unique way that I've never before encountered. Where did you get the inspiration for this one? No matter, an excellent poem.

Stretching Roads

  XX, you have excelled with this poem. I see you in it and all the others that have gone before you and will come after you... walking this particular stretch of road. The message and emotion transcends the words. One of your finest poems, thus far, in my opinion.

Wine Clothing

A most intriguing poem, XX. I find this one having a complex bouquet of emotion, color and temperature. There are many dimensions... a sort of tapestry... art, really. I think this one will be read over again and again; many times

Withering Kindness

"Sunflowers are poets willing to die for their art..." ~ you encourage me to embrace the thought. Perhaps that's the way they would have wanted to be remembered rather than languishing, less appreciated and left to wither among their kind. Do suppose it possible that some of them are now in you and they... endure in that way, in some unknown measure?

Embarrassed Vous

Ominous and seductive at the same time... very good. I like your choice of imagery too; both types. I could go on about home as much I like this but that would just embarrass you, right? ☺

Word Heaps

Heh! Yes, rummaging around in the heap-o-words can be serendipitous. But it takes a good scrounger to find the treasure in the trash; I'm betting on your horse, XY. ☺

Serious Suckage

I get it... and the message is worthy but the grammar just sucks. Work on it. Please. I'm sure you have much to offer the world but your English language skills need work. Seriously. You can feel free to break the rules for the sake of poetic art with impunity but only after you've learned the basics. Other than that, it's a fine poem and I liked it. Thank you! ☺

Asexual Worms

Lyrical, pastoral and pleasingly balanced but did you know... there are worms that don't need another worm to reproduce? ...just saying. ☺

Shouting Winds

Ominous, what one may read between the lines... the visions that come dancing, flickering between stanzas, between lines that reveal the deepest, darkest secrets of the inner psyche. The brush strokes, like finger prints, meet at critical junctures and align each word with its corresponding passion. How fortunate we call it poetry. Imagine other venues of interpretation where the proforma thoughts delegate unwanted villas in the style of a dark tomb. No beaches here. No wind or shouts of youthful laughter. "...time to go." Thankfully, this gallery is well-lighted and out of the weather. You are quite the artist, XY.

Industrial Retreats

Honestly, I didn't look at the title or subtitle before I started reading and I thought the piece was about a door-mat. I got to the second stanza and then I began wondering what sort of door mat would have:

... a back with a thousand turns and jumps;a face full of hair and eyes like a hanging Jesus.

Needless to say the next two stanzas tipped me off balance and then threw an uppercut to the jaw. Once I regained my balance it was plain that I was outmatched. I surrendered to the nature of that prismatic lensing of cinematic perfection - that "...tearing of bread under a rain of feathers."

Then, I am squarely at odds with the humanistic dogma that follows: "...he prays and eats to love..." A rabbit punch to the kidneys. (Sorry, you have a fox, I a rabbit.) I slip into unconsciousness with the final blow, like the fox, I too retreat into that "...shocked hole of silence."

This is a different kind of poetry. I'm going to call it post-modern industrial; with your permission of course. Unless you prefer something else?

Balanced Legacies

I had written something reasonable. Perhaps even well-intentioned... but the random demons that infest this realm of karmic-bound writers decided that it was my turn to be consumed for a breakfast of meager punishments for some past misdeed. Having no winder-back in my possession it is impossible to draw the same water from the well twice.

So, I start afresh with a new drink... sipping in silence while rereading and thinking of the keys to this piece:

"Suzanne, guileless at thirteen... we... unconscious of our natural part in the scheme of things" "...the butterflies have it right - with their magnetic stuff of life"

It was something about envy for your reading glasses. Perhaps the ones you wear when writing about these pieces of life that seem filtered by them in a way that encourages memory to pass through only those things that support and affirm that sense of balance and of right-with-world enduring upon which the very best of legacies are built.

Chapter 14

Inside Prize

Sleep - the great escape - that unaware remembering...

"memory trespasses at will, penetrating this limbo... let me sip Lethe's nectar... just not today."

For some, these are the years of rice and salt. The bardo awaits each for that sorting of deeds and desires. My journal entries as a child were like thoughts on a cereal box compared to this - the prize inside. [BTW, at your tickling, I have some things for you to read. ☺]

Rocket Sprockets

For some strange reason I see a diorama... and keep thinking of Futurama... Bender and robot sex... no, that would be machines having sex... but are machines conscious while having sex? Who cares... all those plungers, valves, sprockets and sockets – if we keep on like this... Ooops. Sorry. Didn't mean to break your rocket. Never mind. ☺

Speaking Volumes

Oh, I disagree with your author's note that claims you "know nothing of hermit crabs." This piece is very much and insight into the mental workings of those shoreline denizens; as evidenced by their behaviors - and some people that mimic aspects of their existence. For me, a humorous, wry piece that speaks volumes to those with the years to discern the truth in it. Well done, XY. Well done.

Couples Senses

Wow! Just an opinion mind you but I think this one _is_ both inspired and beautiful; really, truly uuly. I doff my solar visor in honor of you, the goddess of inspiration (there is one, isn't there?) and Thor's Day. Whereas some may sense longing in this, I do not. I read it as a "what is - now"; coupled with a sense of the enduring or perhaps a vision of what may yet come to pass. Anyway it's read it is still lovely. Kudos, XX! ☺

Beer Buckets

Here's to beer and the thoughts it can produce when gazing about those passionless roosts... in a tavern in a town sits a bucket, nice and round... around it's rim a blue tail fly - to the bucket of fermenting suds it thinks, "Should we be lovers?" with a sigh.

Toga Washers

Ah, a piece of philosophical whimsy! ☺ So where is that "life force" in that strawberry now? Do we value the patterns of our consciousness more than the medium of expression? You, XY, have kicked the hornets nest, stolen fire from the gods and rush toward the temples with a basket of dusty fruit. Let's hope the toga washers will prosper.

Rushing Spoons

Mmmm... yes... even a silver-spoon existence in paradise becomes a lesser place if we have no one to share it with. The deft balance, the five-fold starfish symmetry of this piece; teeter-tottering on the afternoon. Each arm a textured montage of routine seeking harmony and finding only a dissonant sadness; reflected in that one drying plate. Words of enchanted lineage that reveal one simple truth... so elegantly. Do you feel the rush of honest admiration? This is a great one, XX.

Other Layers

This is quite a basket of derivatives, XY. In the sense that many of the words and phrases derive from primitives and in turn spawn yet other layers of expressive passion. Such a tease... such a nicely written tease. ☺

Simple Savages

You have the right of it I think. That last stanza pretty much says it all, doesn't it? ... and you expressed it so very well; captured the essential nuance of the positions between combatant and observer with, as you put it, "savage simplicity." Excellent, XY.

Photo Floods

My, my, my... this is simply overflowing with imagery! I was so smitten with them that I tried to composite everything that it contained - selecting those images that seemed to fit the mood and style of your piece. It's too bad I can't paste it here. You might enjoy it... as much as I enjoyed the poem. ☺ I'll put a copy in my photo album here. Feel free to peruse/borrow if you so desire.

Tender Morsels

I trust it was received well? It is certainly dramatic... and the elements of torment seem teasingly subdued, as though that reflection of inner-self is playing with a young and tender morsel. It would not hold such pathos if it were old decaying flesh. The final verse is epic irony, pressed flat in leaves of future pages yet to be written. All said, well said, nicely done - this one.

Chapter 15

Whole Halves

As clear and deadly as the inside of Pandora's box. Perhaps a translation from the Voynich manuscript if it were translatable in this place and time. Clearly you are skilled in telling half-wholes, XY, nicely too.

Limp Laundry

Very good! This one has a common reach down into the depths of everyone's closet box; the one with those long-forgotten pictures that bring back an avalanche of memories – those "what ifs and why nots." I like this one a lot. How on earth do you keep writing these things and not go a little crazy? I'd be limp laundry, hung out to dry, ready for the loony drive-by hooting; especially at the pace you write.

Growing Conflictions

At four years old, it's hard to comprehend that sort of stuff. We just know who is nice and who is not; who makes us laugh, feeds us, tucks us in to bed with kisses and stories – and who does just the opposite. It's an easy choice for most. Why does the dog bite the hand that feeds it? Probably because the foot it's attached to kicks it. What child wouldn't grow up conflicted? A poem to ponder at all levels. Thanks XX.

Jumping Juices

I now have a bad case of mental tongue pretzels! Sheesh, XY... it's awfully hard to laugh properly with ones diction tied in knots!! Good thing I was able manage a couple of snorts else I might have exploded. What on earth got into your pen? Jumping juice?? ☺

Pained Existence

Sometimes I think you write these things just for me. Is that weird or what?! :) I suppose I do sort of put you (your work = you, right?) under a microscope for the first couple of reading iterations of a new piece but then I usually step back and try to see "the big picture." There are other times when I think, based upon what you write and how your write it, that you actually are quite happy in that "dustless and utterly untouchable" place; it's so safe there, isn't it? I'm sure there really is a part of you that longs to be released from the necessity of absorbing the world from behind that single-paned existence... but if you didn't do it that way (some of the time) you just wouldn't be you... and that's why we all love you.

Bondage Forms

I'm trying to understand the imagery ... the only time I have seen a dove near the surface of water is when they are drinking; perhaps from a mud puddle or other. So, you may be talking about a reflection. The poem speaks of a lopsided relationship, of a sort of battle or struggle... {finishes eating ice cream cone} oh, this is most curious. You see, there are not a lot of "emo" words used; only "love" and "fought." Although you did repeat it twice - to drive the point home or to provide a symmetry/balance of sorts. That "she" is a "dove" is important - four times the image of the symbolic dove, of a "her." She is the thinker, the possible chattel since she is his; but he is not hers - a possessive relationship - an immature relationship based upon a naive sense of "ownership." Perhaps an ownership that is unwarranted and unwanted in the sense that it is not based upon the lasting essentials of mutual affection and respect. The remainder... words of contemplation for a reader; she is cerebral, thinking, perhaps submissive where he plays her like an instrument. And though she knows this, it is the price of the bond - a form of bondage and servitude. And yet she knows but wants the world to know she knows... and so we do.

A very simple yet intriguing poem with much to savor and think about.

Inadequate Protections

A loaf of bread, a jug of wine and thou beside me - scribbling in the wilderness. You call the bees that sting with the honey that drips from your lips, XY. How should I encourage your precocious nature? With what tint should I varnish the beautiful striations of your sonorous violin? Should I hear this symphony anew or perchance lilting through daring caravans I might consider raising an umbrella to the sky - even though it be inadequate protection from this dark showering.

Spider Weavings

This place where you go to survey the damage; a place painted in relationships knit together by emotion and expectations. A place where words are used both as building materials and as implements of destruction... a not-yet sanctuary for something that masquerades as love and causes the objectified sacrifice to struggle at unseen bonds; struggle for an ideal of freedom. One wonders if a solution or reparations is both possible or forthcoming? An excellent construction of deftly woven connectives. My compliments to both you and the spider; you for writing and it for giving you the inspiration.

Glass Pieces

The Ad reads... "For Sale: One million shattered glass pieces. A wide variety of colors. Excellent for various art projects such as mosaics and stained glass. Or remelt in kiln to form art nouveau glass shapes. See table for shipping and handling." Any love-starved artist would see this as an opportunity to take those dangerous broken pieces and put them into a blazing heart - to be melted into something beautiful again.

Prize Winners

In your stuff... in this piece... It's impossible for the naked eye to see but I feel there are tiny little cuts, here and there so that the words, lines, stanzas are like a sort of magnetic poetry set. In my mind I move them about by just reading in various directions; left, right, up, down, diagonal, etc.. It's amazing what falls out, drops out, hops out, sprints out and runs slobbering for the big red button near the sign on the wall, the one labeled "Escape Pod." E.g.: "What if I wish to forget midnight for cotton candy?" The wheel of fortune spins, that clicking sound, those spaces lighting up so the winning contestant solves the puzzle. A phrase from a famous poem by the founding father of the poetic school of Neonoetics, "What A Joke, or 12:01." One can only wonder at the taxes levied on those prize winners.

Understanding Glimpse

Wow! ... to read it again would be to double-deep the scar, the brand that it leaves. Should we pity the reader that may glimpse and understanding? Is it not an end that comes to all born to this realm of times? Perhaps you write to believe what is written in your heart and in so doing "...comes the dawn."

Chapter 16

Surviving Tolerance

I think this piece is terribly, horribly inspired, XX. The thought-environment spawned by this sweltering write... a steaming heat that simmers the heart's sense of fair play and produces an uncomfortable perspiration of exasperation. It frames a playing field where rules of inequitable interaction are in force; so lacking in give-&-take or perhaps that extra measure of tolerance and compassion; so necessary for any relationship that would survive. In the end it leaves this reader wondering about "it", about the future and choices and how that the life of that "good girl" may yet unfold. Tantalizing and deeply unsatisfying... such is the message for me or did I miss the point?

Dining Whims

The blue fire illumines now and... how is it that you have looked at my life and summarized it so succinctly and ... with such gruesome grace? This fair scribble, of hobbit hilt, should n'er be played w'out a kilt and pipes to lure the mourners in... to this room of memories playing their dark melodic din; for those that live upon the tip of whims dine enchanted by your skimming pen. ~ Anon.

Trusty Ships

See XY!!? ...and you thought that you would only be a footnote; that even the history as told by sand worms or hooter monkeys would turn a blind eye to you and your work. XY has immortalized you in the style of Forniclaise (branded deep within the glaze)! Your story is now legend - carved into the gangplank railing of the HMSS Cafe Grande! Ring the bell, thrice... the Captain speaks, "Let those that board this trusty ship experience the texture of his passage upon their bared extremities! Huzzah!"

Careful Weighings

Hi XX! This is an interesting topic for a poem. It's probably just as well that you and your mother never engaged one that could actually perform as advertised. I like your poem a lot simply because you honestly state what most people feel/think about the subject in general and by default its various nooks and crannies. But the world is so much stranger than we can imagine. I'll just leave you with this... if you ever think you've met someone (or something) that actually is pretty good at answering your "beyond the veil" future-looking questions - weigh carefully your need-to-know and be careful of what you ask. That sort of knowledge always has a price associated with it that is never clearly stated.

Red Flowers

In times past, in similar circumstance, I have assumed a form of prostration before such beauty and sought to embrace that expose of tenderness and beg a small memory-token of the spirit within; perhaps a deep-drawn breath of fragrance or a touch of velvet form. The morose mood of this piece's epode casts a form of pall, a dark and despairing shadow. I am saddened to imagine that single red flower, plucked from its sacred alter; perhaps crying to the earth mother in its final moment of existence, "...forget me not."

Shallow Wading

And you were complaining of "wading in the shallows?!" Honestly, this is like listening to a mythic tale, told with the voice of a dual-throated Fury intent upon affixing an imposing a well-deserved time out upon a writer that has dared to violate their muse's sacred trust by relieving themselves in the Eternal Well-spring of All Inspiration. I am cringing and trying to slink away before I'm noticed. ⊛ Awesome write! Totally awesome!!

Monopole Memes

Honestly, I would never have believed that a poem could come from such a novel concept. If I have it by the short hairs then this is surely about an addiction for confliction. I am forced to see these goosebumps marching in parade ground formation, illumined from the sidelight and magnified by a simple glass-loop dropping of heady sarong sweat. The fourth stanza surely supports this thesis: seductive intentions are just place holders for an imagination that is insulting itself because of what it imagines. Wow! That's like turning a stomach inside out to see if it's done digesting. And that last stanza... well, that's just off the wall - and at that point I imagined the tone arm on the platter scratching to center by an unseen force. Keep this up and we're going to need new methods of mental calibration and instrumentation to compare these monopole poeto-magnetic memes, XY old man.

Compass Stars

A wonderful piece, XX. Take heart, even a "lost compass" will point true in the absence of an iron mass of uncaring influence. Let him rust. Twinkle, sparkle in the sunlight so that another, more curious and caring passer-by will notice the charm of your reflections. Let new hands take your compass and together chart the stars anew in this dark expanse of life.

Weaving Worlds

An exceptionally brilliant lament, XX. How long indeed; perhaps time has little meaning for such rhetorical questions, true? They stand aside and watch the world weave the fabric of itself.

Silken Lamentations

Slingshot curios rat-a-tat against wizened, callous sentiment. Ladles full of ipecac protect and coat this curious mordant phrasing. It slithers across the page with the grace of a centipede intent upon karmic fluid that can sate its ravenous pursuit. Who will bless the needy, suspended in drunken contemplation within this zone of comprehensive desolation? I wonder and marvel at the magnificence of your silken lamentations, oh XY!

Chapter 17

Harsh Clarity

Oh, this is a sad place to be. I hear you. I understand, at least from my perspective; there's probably an overlap. As writing it's clear and searing. As a strategy it's workable but harsh. It may not be as bad as it seems. But, you probably don't want advice; just acknowledgment, right? Good poem too for what it's worth.

Controlling Illusions

There is a species of bird, ducks I think (I saw it on TV), they nest high up on sheer cliffs. When the young have hatched and out-grown the nest they jump... often hundreds of feet; some land near the water's edge and some upon the rocks. It's amazing to see those that hit the rocks, bounce and then scramble toward the water and join their siblings that are following their mother to finish the rest of their lessons before becoming fully functional and independent. A controlling parent is either overly fearful and protective or distracted by their own lives; which is it here?

Untouched Mysteries

Anyone? No? OK, then I will say it... marvelous! "For us time is irrelevant..." XX, this is really one of your very best. It is certainly one of my favorites to date. I can't elaborate on what you've done or how you did it because it's a delightful mystery to me. I am content, as Iris says, to let the mystery be.

Harsh Realities

I agree with the rest... a great poem. It's the honest sentiment of a harsh reality. Intentional or not, you seemed to have captured the vodka-like slur, here and there. That slight-of-hand magic trick really sold the piece for me. Having said that and heaped you with great praise I feel that I'm permitted to ask the burning question: Were you actually drunk when you wrote this?

Borrowed Hankies

I love the opening lines. I'm still trying to remember, exactly, the smell of wet asphalt; there are different kinds you know. I don't understand the latter part of the second stanza: a lament is interrupted in order to ignore some sounds. The middle is somewhat cognitive/dissociative; although I did appreciate the"mosquito-buzzing torture of a singed heart" - that rocks! So does the paper cup words.

As for the last, I tend to agree with XX. You probably wouldn't want to borrow my hanky. I think it reeks of horse snot.

Telling Selves

What, no humor? ... a studied afternoon, in the style of a Victorian dowager that reads H.P. Lovecraft. I surrender to the piece and allow it to tell me what it wants in order to tell itself. Having boiled it down, it seems to weep about what was left out. The triumph of killers that smile with glee at having stolen the souls of all those paper dolls. And yet the parallelism is a triumph of secrets. Kudos to those that run with the rounded scissors! ☺

Spectral Cupboards

I hear you. It's post-modern reflective; in a good way. It takes a certain kind of audience but, hey, I'm sure you've found a sample here and rest assured, they know it's an articulate commentary put into a delicate prose that fits well into that special place in our mental cupboards. The one right next to the "status happy." The muses embrace you, XX! ☺

Dead Gardens

What an exquisitely beautiful way to say it! "I'm not sorry your gone but I do miss some of those things you did." Yes, those affections we ply upon our friends and companions; in the hope that such nurturing will bear the fruit of true love. But, even a dead garden can retain a certain beauty and memory of the lush bounty of its season; as you have written so well in this piece, XX. Nicely done! ☺

Surreal Moments

Escapism, rendered clearly, harshly and without pity or remorse. It is left to the reader to understand "who" and "what"; that's as it should be, this reflection of shared moment for those to which it applies. Another enduring snapshot of surreal moments looking through finger-frames at a contemporary existence. Nicely done, XX.

Cannibal Wheels

Excellent! I like everything about the way that you've rendered this vicious cycle of love's longing for equal attraction, followed by disenchantment, disillusionment and feelings of hopeless abandonment. The format is supporting and well-crafted too. A worthy poem, XX.

Chapter 18

Caring Curves

If you want someone to "care" then you need to (try and) understand that the word means different things to different people. The important thing is what it means to you. So, what does it mean? How do/will you know if someone actually cares about you? Will it change you? Will it change your life? Why was is/was it important to you... to someone else... to anyone? Someone can say they love you and they can hug you, provide for you, fawn all over you but what's the difference between those actions and simply "caring" about someone? Now ask yourself, what is the difference between caring and love?

Moon Tugs

If we drink honey every day then how can we know the sweetness of water? If I am a brick maker then should I make everything of brick? Or should we rather consider the oceans and how each drop is only water and yet unique unto itself? Draw a circle in the sand on the beach... what is different about the sand inside that particular circle? Do we discern the sand, the circle or the difference? What then when moon tugs at the waves and they, gently touching the beach, send the circle home? Where is home? Where is XX's star?

Movie Clips

OK, I think I've got it... it's like "The Producers" meets "Dr. Who", right? :D Un-seriously, you were commending me on my visualization skills (big mistake) so here's what I "saw":

Keep in mind that I know absolutely nothing about this craft but... I saw myself sitting in a rather large theater. Center, a few rows back... where all of the mucky-mucks sit during such rehearsals in the movies (of rehearsals). What I am seeing is the the stage in reverse. In the center of the stage are the curtains as seen from back stage but "scaled down" in order to accommodate the effect. I'm seeing MATTIE and TREVOR and their props (the stool, headset, etc.) on the stage-left quarter of the set. The center 1/2 of the stage is "busy" with behind the scenes activity but (somehow) is not detracting from the dialog of the main characters as they come into focus; probably with some form of lighting, curtains, or other theatrical techniques. Stage-right is reserved for something... not sure what; surprise me! ☺

One neat thing is that the center stage has distant curtain/screen can be used as a form of Kabuki theater to enhance the effects of MATTIE's commands to the various stage crew and actors. At key moments it opens up to reveal a "movie clip" of an audience; applauding, gasping in horror, laughing or whatever seems appropriate for the alien-human, tap dancing dinosaur love fest production-within-a-production.

So, this is really a play about life imitating art imitating life... did I get that right? ☻

——— errata: Mattie: Well, Act II is much shorter than Act II. ~ Um, which is shorter?! errata: being so prejudice against the alien ~ prejudiced

———

I thank you, profusely, for (re)writing it so that's it's readable by normal people. I'm sure that the formats for real scripts are necessary and extraordinarily useful to people that are familiar with them and have to use them in real life/work but, for this non-executive moron the way that you've depicted it, story-like, is absolutely wonderful. It "reads" very well!

I doff my imaginary cap to you, my dearest Lady XX, for such a wonderful play (and a smashing good read). I agree with XY's; this is going to be a success. Pardon me, while I beg and grovel for an invite too or, if you prefer and it's easier, simply an autographed copy of one of the what-ever-they-hand-out thingies!

Big Smiley

There's a fancy word: catharsis. It has several variations of definition but the gist of it, according to an English dictionary, is the purging and renewal of emotion through some form of external expression such as "art." I suppose writing is an art. Most writer's like to think so. Having read "The story of you and me" it seems that you should be due for a moment of catharsis; anytime now. Do you like virtual hugs? {hug} The next time you treat yourself to a meal, dining out, on the off chance that you're alone... try to think of this enigmatic avatar with a big smiley face on it, sitting across the table from you, lifting a glass of something and saying, "Here's to you and the rest of your life, XX! Now, let's eat... I'm starved."

Sandy Hoots

Well, well... I wrote this long "thing", my usual interpretations, you know, but I'm reluctant to besmirch your nice page with it. I let it set for a couple of hours and it sprouted a sort of icky mold. You can still have it if you want it. ☺

That said, I'm pretty sure history will find a good place for you and your work. Something a little more prominent than a footnote. Sheesh! Give yourself a little credit, OK? Of course it may be the history as told by sand worms or hooter monkeys but hey, it's all good, right? ☺

Jelly Babies

Hmmm.... I think your writer-in-residence was taken with the "taste" of your words. I believe it's hard for most people to connect a word with the sense of taste; especially ones that are not flavors from their usual menu. The connectives are reasonable though somewhat elusive. I've wanted to try this too; as an experiment of course. For example, what would you say if I said that this poem has a sense of Southwestern seasoning; a churro? At least that's the way it starts but then I'm teleported to somewhere in Jersey or perhaps Hogwarts where I get a taste of Earwax flavored jelly babies and then step into Dr. Who's Tardis for a trip to WW-I and the French country cuisine taste of cold mud-blood-rain soup. We need to work on contrast and presentation. They say it's best to consider the dish and then match the color of the service for best contrast. For this piece, I'd go with a simple white. Perhaps square or other line geometry; not circular. There's nothing smooth and relaxing going on here. Then either chop sticks or 3-tine silver; not stainless. This is definitely not stainless. I'm stumped though by what to serve beyond the chilled ice water. To contrast the dour mood perhaps something from a happy gamay grape? Yes, that might go well with the trench water soup.

My friend, you are (and by default, your work is) a marvelous provocateur of my silly penchant for odd verbosity and interpretive fantasies. Thank you! ☺

Open Hearts

XX, I just want to say that this is most refreshing writing. I started at the bottom and read them all; one after the other. They drew me into your perspective and let me see through your eyes. Your sentiments, while familiar, were your own and unique. But they became mine too as I read you. This is a wonderful thing. To be able to write, to express what you are thinking and feeling in a manner that does not cause the reader to cringe or shy away. And there was no shying away. You opened your heart, your bedroom, your life, even parts of the closet where you keep those dark secrets that you can/will only allude to in your writing.

Rhetoric Dogs

Yes! Yes, this is how we slip into madness. But what is that but another facet of who we really are. Surrounded by everyone and alone, in a sea of thoughts, we drown. Why does pasta without the sauce look so strange? Oh, never mind. What's in a review? Did I read it? Yes. Did I like it. Yes. Did it get me all riled up? No. Should it have? ...ya got me there. Poke me harder next time; maybe I'll cry or just shut up and kiss me... I'm kinda shy. I agree, let's leave the rest to the rest. Did you hear that clink in the tin cup? Is it tipping the organ grinder's monkey or a golf ball SFX of a hole in one? Does someone have a dog named Rhetoric? I'd like to know. Wouldn't you?

Hand Washers

Yeah, this is a keeper. The real key is the differentiation of intangibles. The objects you choose to hover over with magnifying glass and tweezers appear, occasionally, as explanatory confabulations; expect when they're not. Who's to say for sure? Well, there's the mystery of it, isn't it? A curtsy of the kilt to this fine gold-fingered blue-marbled hand washer of tale. Fish tale? ...hmm.

Chapter 19

Splitting Rails

Isn't it nice that you can write something like this and live to tell/publish your thoughts? It is my understanding, some admittedly based upon second hand accounts, that there are other countries, ethnic regions, or religious domains where you would likely suffer for it. Perhaps greatly.

Here, in the northern hemisphere of the Americas, the worst that will probably happen is that this poetic commentary will be read and then be ignored. I doubt that's what you intend or hope for but, in my opinion, that is the likely outcome.

Oh, you are not alone. There are many who found, and still do find, it fashionable to rail against "the establishment"; the evils of many governments and business are known worldwide and are legendary... and history shows us that these evils can be found in any century.

In my opinion, one of the best measures of the worth of any society is how much and to what extent they stifle the voices of opposition for or against any given topic/subject. I challenge you to consider this measure in the context of what forces are necessary to bring it about, to birth it as it were, and maintain it for any length of time.

Perhaps then you may find some discriminators of judgment (or inspiration) that were overlooked or ill considered in the pursuit of truth and/or expounding upon the compassion of the human spirit.

Keep in mind that this is not an attack upon you personally or upon your work or an attempt to sway you from whatever position or convictions you may have with respect to the content of this poem. Rather it is a brief commentary upon the thoughts and subject of this piece.

The poem itself is excellent. Thank you for sharing, XY.

Vintage Years

If a I may be so bold... It's like you almost wanted to say something truly deep and meaningful but at the very end you chickened out. I can't imagine why. You haven't been particularly shy lately. I suppose if there is something in the window worth pausing to gawk at it must the delicate way this knot, this almost-relationship, was undone. Even forbidden wine must have its preferred vintage years. What matter the few scratches incurred in traversing the garden, the vineyard; it's all about the tasting with this one, isn't it?

Closet Cleaners

Optimistic minstrel, singing with a hint of determined sentimentalism... a sense of pioneer adventurer too... with a touch of western landscape artist turned agronomist thrown in for good measure. You should turn out your closet more often. ☺

Hungry Mornings

{stomp, stomp, stomp} ... it is I, Bigfoot. I've come to caress your bottle of syrup for I have pancakes and butter to contribute. Thank you for sharing! I shall not hunger this morning. Oh, look! A fly, right there, in your orange juice. Oh my...

Mocking Birds

Bird, descendant of the dinosaur, mocks man with it's gift of flight. But, woman's imagination overtakes it with a thought. And in that instant all history is undone for the sun is made in her image.

Keyed Memories

I didn't have to search far... in this age all knowledge is as near as memory's key. This quote, stolen from modern scribes (and with great gusto) lays better claim to a suitable response and review than any that I might fashion from my own dim wit.

"There are conflicting accounts of Diogenes' death. He is

alleged variously to have held his breath; to have become ill from eating raw octopus;[30] or to have suffered an infected dog bite.[31] When asked how he wished to be buried, he left instructions to be thrown outside the city wall so wild animals could feast on his body. When asked if he minded this, he said, "Not at all, as long as you provide me with a stick to chase the creatures away!" When asked how he could use the stick since he would lack awareness, he replied "If I lack awareness, then why should I care what happens to me when I am dead?""

Word Mobiles

This is the very best collection of sayings taped together that I have ever read. They make a marvelous mobile of words, spinning around there in the air.

Wild Rides

I feel... like it was a great roller-coaster write! ☺ The take off was smooth and polite but the middle was scary with those wild antithetical gyrations. However, in the end, I was able to get off the ride and walk straight without falling down. Let's do it again!! ☻

Wanting Take-out

I hear the theme music from the TV show "Twilight Zone" (USA, 1960s, SciFi) somewhere in the background but it's seem like the melody is a bit off; like it's been mutated for this clandestine satellite channel that I've just tuned in on my under-the-counter converter box. It's a strange episode. Like the one of the homicidal ventrilo-quist's dummy but without the homicide and without the dummy; sort of like that. I'm somewhat surprised by the ending. Surprised that this toy designer doesn't harness more of that creative energy and upgrade his doll face. Perhaps the next episode? Sadly, there is no guide for this channel, for this type of programming. I'll just have to keep watching and waiting... that goodness the place around the corner delivers. At least I won't starve.

Perfecting Achievement

I can see you were inspired and tried hard to reach just the right embodiment in words. But, as we all eventually realize, perfection is only an ideal. A goal to be sought, by some, with the understanding that it may never be achieved.

Redwood Whispers

It sparkles with "the life she was meant to have." Perhaps thinking she could "own" it was, in some way, an admis-sion of understanding for why it was not (yet) so? Who can hold a drop of water suspended between thumb and finger and not yearn? The magic of memory, the enchantments of childhood, will always render impossibly perfect land-scapes. This canvas is rendered in the palette of thought; with colors that the softest sable is unable to fully retain. It is a wonderful wind chime sun-catcher of words and the existential ending follows nicely in the moon's shadow.

Chapter 20

Eros Goodbyes

I'm enjoying the new/old Leica look. It frames the depth
of your inkwell with a certain kind of petulant symmetry.
For every coming there must be a going out otherwise the
universe is without motion. The expectations of princesses
are above the lonely, sad little frogs that line the splendor
of your constellation, croaking in every sense at the demise
of ardor and their abandonment by Eros.

Thoughtless Acts

Yes, sometimes it happens that way, doesn't it? Those
kids we play with when we're young and living in-the-
moment. There is no thought of them as hamburger in car
wrecks, as cripples from incurable disease, as body-scarred
victims of a single thoughtless acts or undeniable screams
fleeing the memories of war. There is a word for this kind of
memory, this kind of writing: poignant. It is the accidental

touch of the grill upon bare flesh as the mind wanders, contrasting it's good fortune to those that cannot be there to share. But, they're here now, in some fashion, through this. Perhaps there's a thank you in the wind for you; a thank you for remembering and sharing.

Screaming Voices

I guess I'll provide some counterpoint.

I've never liked that painting. Not because of the color, style or skill of the artist but rather because of the multitude of possibilities that are all too apparent in both representation and message. "The Scream" portrays a human cry; something people are wont to do out of desperation when all other possibilities for relief fail. It represents all too well that universal plea for help while, simultaneously, signaling unequivocal surrender to forces that have upset a delicate balance – so necessary for existence in the often harsh reality of the human experience.

This piece, this poem, provides an abstract interpretive voice that supports the basic theme of the painting. A clear rendering of details that would perhaps go unnoticed; branches of thought unimagined by the more casual viewer.

I admire the form, phrasing and verbal imagery. I am intrigued with the subject of the painting's voice and imagined thoughts that provide even deeper levels of between-the-lines pensive laments. Still, I remain disturbed by the implications of a personal interpretation and resonance. For me, it has accomplished the goal of poetry. I do not turn the page unscathed.

Touching Wires

You love me. I know you do. Don't deny it. I can tell because you keep using those certain words over and over again. The same ones that drill tiny holes in the woodwork box where I live. Then you serenely place those sparkling jewels of starlight onto gossamer strings and suspend them in such a way and place that I am forced to reach out for them... that whole moth-to-light thing (you know what I'm talking about.) I don't mind if I die and "disintegrate into a pile of dust" - that's and appropriate end for those who dare to stand in water and then touch the wires of electric genius.

Shifting Technologies

Very nice! The contrasts of hue & saturation juxtaposition; substitutions of image and emotion. For a moment there it was old tech versus new; an old 35mm Leica shooting B&W film then contrasted with a color digital image on a retina display. The instant time travel of decades in timeless moments.

Fleeting Plaudits

It is unnecessary for the anvil to be prepared to meet the hammer. It was made for this purpose and is not alive. Do you think the human soul, as intangible as the feelings of an anvil and hammer, must be prepared to meet life? If yes, then why is there always the expectation and fear of life's uncertainty? If no, then the same question.

Should poetry be pragmatic, always? Can it be less or more at a whim? There are as many answers as thinkers of thoughts. Who can know the true meaning of the words a poet writes? The truth is elusive, relative, fleetingly enduring.

This is not a review. It is commentary; elicited from reading your fine poem. I thought it might interest you and serve a more noble purpose than plaudits.

Ripe Recollections

There is something really strange going on here, with your writing that is... and I'm going crazy trying to figure it out (the variance). Although it is obvious that this piece is in the same style and mindset as 'A Long Time Ago, Now', it is markedly different. This one sets the orchestration immediately and then opens the first movement quickly with a trio of object-instruments that sound that opening, dominant chord. The word-tone palette too is set in the first stanza and carries forth throughout. Perhaps it is the rhythm of the temporal constructions; the memory accents that enhance those "flashes that dictate dreaming" as the supporting thought-instruments appear and lend their carefully placed support for the overarching design of the composition? The end stanza carries your signature service setting of silvered human components, carefully aged in dark mnemonic casks and poured out for a repast of ripe recollection.

Unsavory Reflections

It is so sad; how you write the truth with such young blooded words. Keep in mind that the truth has many facets; from sparkle, to blinding glare or simply a dull reflection. If you don't like what you see then just walk about until the view changes to something more pleasing. Personally, I don't think it's possible to dwell for any length of time in a place of perpetual bliss. Even if we stop at that point where it's good for us it will, most certainly, move about us until we are no longer where we thought we were. It is a pragmatic and perhaps unsavory view of how the soul may transcend life but, perhaps, a necessary one.

Wounded Pigeons

As a communique of the heart it struggles. Like a pigeon wounded while traversing enemy lines we see it gain altitude in places and drop in others. Taking advantage of those serendipitous up drafts caused by the flames of passion it struggles across a no-man's-land of thought, descending with that inevitable downward arc toward and untimely death in some muddy trench of memory. Alas, in creative inspiration there are always casualties – always collateral damage.

Sentimental Seasoning

I like this vignette and mood study. Your choice of word-paint renders a small portrait of eventuality with a keen sense of balance between the light and dark aspects of emotional baggage attached to the physical accouterments of life. An activity of contemporary existence bound tightly to the material-seeking society of this age. The sentimental seasoning gives this literary bisque just the right punch too; something to sauce up the highlight for the reader when they reach maximal correlation as they draw water from their own well of existence.

New Worlds

This piece seems to be a form of mending message. Perhaps descendant from an "in vivo" review of those "histrionics" that often lead to a mild writer psychosis. The voice of the italic lines seem to support this possibility with their counterpoint of persona-voice swings; the ghost of he who has physically left the stage but is still present by his apparent absence. But the use of this mechanism appears inconsistent because there is a sense that the italic voice is not always the same consciousness; and yet, we know it must be the authors, shifting subtly from one mental POV to the next. In one counterpoint it is the voice of "him", in the next it is inconclusive but could be someone else yearning for that creative space between waking and sleep while in the third the heart of the explorer unrolls that map, purchased in some dark alley of the mind, with thoughts of acquiring backers for a voyage to the new world that lies just over the horizon.

Dismal Weather

Ah, gentle, fluttering allegory. Perhaps we look for light because the day IS so discouraging? Although... I've heard it attributed frequently to dismal British weather.

Chapter 21

Buoyant Laughs

I like it. Really. Now, let it be known that I am ever so much more interested in you writing a (very) short story about a "low-life swamp rat!" This would give you a little more freedom to engage your imagination without being concerned with poetic form. Or perhaps a free-verse poem about those low-life swamp rats? Sorry, I guess I'm just enamored with the entertainment value of someone writing something about low-life swamp rats; not to diminish your pain or anything. Sometimes it's helpful to poke fun at a situation. The laughter can often provide a spiritual buoyancy that tends to lift one out of the ruts you speak of.

Dense Journeys

Heh! So, this begins where Asimov ends and then transcends the blend of fuddy duddy muddy study. It must be a requisite skill, or at least a useful trait of poets; to be able to turn idle distractions into erudite commentary that dispels any fear of learning unwanted knowledge that may, some day, be useful in a conversation with an entomophobic friend. How sad that college science (Entomology) texts do not intersperse their dense foliage with lines such as these. It would make the journey ever so much more pleasant (not to mention entertaining).

Joy Mongers

Magnificent!!! Have you been peeking again?! ☺ Ah, to entertain thoughts of the goddess in all women... time surrenders in those moments. I've rediscovered a word that I think fits moments like these: resplendent. Oh, and joy mongering. I like that too because that's pretty much what this is. Just good o'le fashioned joy mongering. ☺

Dressing Rooms

Well put. An excellent descriptor of that brief moment in the temporal existence play. That snippet about learning, well, that's just another manifestation of the grand mystery of it all, isn't it? The desire to make some sense of the lines we've spoken on the stage as the spotlight upon us "wanes", the stage darkens and we exit as the curtain falls. Afterward, there's nothing left except to go back to the dressing room and wait for the reviews.

Life Sparks

If I thought that you lived in a cardboard box in the back of some dreary alley then this might offer some resistance. As it is, your promiscuity with the word trellis and your proximity to that stage of curving dawn inject a panoramic, smelly view of the ocean. It draws the bulk of the whale herders out as conditions permit. I note that only the more stalwart or disciplined brave the morn and display their "joie de vivre", as you put it, their self-imposed regimens that display their class with a regularity that you can set a watch by; well, that's the essence of that lot anyway. As always, you add a spark to our life, XY. May you never run short of ink.

I guessed wrongly but enjoyed immensely the opportunity to babble with the birds of dawn. ☺

Struggling Thoughts

I think, not as derogatory or detraction, that there is a potential to experience such anguish in the reading of this. Each stanza opens with movement; the movement of limits, of an ascending asymptotic destination that may/will/can never be reached. It struggles and strains against desire and reason while being driven inexorably onward by those same forces. The tension, at times, can be almost unbearable.

To know/experience, if only for a moment, something of a perfect love and then have it "consumed" ... can that word even do justice to the implication of this narrative? I struggle with that thought.

Encrypted Visions

The intro, "Life after life after...", smacks of reincarnation. (I make no judgment on the precept one way or the other.) There is a clear faith present; faith in the thought that those things that need doing will get done and a faith in the place of humanity for such things in the Cosmic All. I like the way you've employed the binary facets of life (the heavens and the firmament) upon an invisible scale that permits the reader a choice to (perhaps inadvertently) lean upon one side or the other (or both). More enigmatic is the stanza beginning with "All the seeds of memory are encrypted..." as it seems to delve more into a personal vision for a certain aspect of immortality. However, in the end, the "oyster" remains affixed to the firmament of its corporeal existence and thus the play, though over, has yet to begin. {curtains}

Tender Depravities

This is chilling. It has that "Silence of the Lambs" feel to it. There is the seed for a good screenplay here too; if you've a mind for that sort of writing/shopping. I can see why you were drawn to the "tender depravity" in my piece now. I don't seek out this sort of writing but if it's good (and this is) then once I've been ensnared I usually follow it through to the end and sigh in relief that it wasn't real... it wasn't me.

Omniscient Attendants

Should you be alarmed that someone will know or may suspect why you wrote this? No. Perhaps not. There is a curious juxtaposition here that is not entirely clear: "...and I will be your Abel." Curious in that it seems a switched-role denial of facts-by-allusion. There is also a gentle, reclusive insanity that pervades the fabric of the lines; the apologetic formality in the manner that words and objects assault the endeared seem only to enhance the effect and the mood. At the end I wonder if I should consider some form of penance for having read a transcript that was/is well suited for the confessional, a priest and the omniscient attendant.

Oozing Lines

Clearly there is a stance, akimbo, a sense of syncopation that is out of sync. This seems a likely candidate or back cover footnote or perhaps the forward to a yet-to-be-written book about (allegorically) plowing the furrows of life from the team perspective. In mule parlance this is learning to "gee & haw" together. However, I find the "Shouldn't we..." lines a bit assumptive; both personally and philosophically. Primarily because these things tend to change over time and there is no acknowledgment of this. However, most readers will not let this distract from the obvious pluck and/or chagrin that ooze from the lines. Welcome to the barn, XX. ☺

Chapter 22

Tetrahedral Firmaments

Two or three reads later there is still much to discern but I think I have a feel for it now. There is the sound, the feel, the shape of a triangle, of things, places, people, feelings; mostly though it is a triangle of feeling. At each corner there is a sense of coupling - of context, history, a lifetime of moments encapsulated in a few well-chosen words that permit all necessary and relevant glimpses from eyes that have been blurred by tears but now see a bit more clearly. This clarity of view pulses with a new-found vibrancy; an affirmation of both self and life that rises up triumphant through a corner of the triad that is now a present presence. An acknowledged balm for latent wounds bound to an ephemeral memory that angled so deeply its point into the heart of the matter. In the end it transcends a two-dimensional tale of loss and abandonment by shooting forth tenacious streamers of hope and love into that starry night. This then provides the stable point of tetrahedral firmament upon which the future is wrought.

Hopeful Voices

I wanted this so much to be a happy ending but I cannot dare to think it yet. There is a shadow of suspense and travail that looms in the distance beyond these lines; those mornings yet to unfold that contain both a dreariness and a sequence of lost spinning-compass moments. Moments framed in an triangle-ocean of morning, noon and night... sodden gasps of consciousness, struggling, beached by waves of anxious dread. Let sleep and dreams provide a map to guide this drifting mote as it navigates the starry mind toward ports of sheltering love. Pray, time, do not abandon this gentle, hopeful voice. It has many yet to call.

Winter Thoughts

It is the vocabulary of shared imagery, of communal imaginings that drip from these stanzas. A simple yet potent cup of words that swirl about in Twilings' depth; good until the last sip when we at last see the portents contained within the remains of that porcelain winter thought. Nicely done, XX.

Undeveloped Pictures

I remember seeing little kittens playing on a polished hardwood floor. They're always slipping and sliding

around, bouncing into things as their savanna genes over-
take common sense during a charge-and-pounce. Thoughts
can be like that so you have a good simile in that first word
and line. The segue from that into "thoughts ...as lyrics"
is, however, a struggle for me. It seems a harsh disconnect
between conceptual environments. The tactile imagery of-
fends the sensibilities; not greatly mind you but there is a
certain degree of discontinuity when the reader must jump
from a general to a writer-specific experiential moment.

As writers, we tend to make assumptions about our readership and their ability to generate a shared context. Without this there can be little in the way of communication.
For example, I do not have the experience, personally, of
frolicking like a monster at night but I do have enough experience with banging about in the night that I can imagine this. But, what embellishment to this does the wind
over waves in moonlight confer upon the action? Now, I'm
seeing monsters on the beach in the moonlight and then...
legs, tangled in the backseat (of a car perhaps?). Is this
a setup for a Sci-Fi thriller? I'm pretty sure it's supposed
to be a mood setup (cue music) where the camera (mind's
eye) draws back from the monsters-beach scene to zoom-
in on the activity in the back seat but... it's yet another
conceptual disconnect. For me at least.

The stanza of tongues-touch-passion-hot-sun-sand-
memories and the branding that prepared the writer (the
voice) for those hard times, when the wind is cold and
people are distant and aloof (colder); these things still
seem to be in aural mode - the lyric sensibility that utters
its complaint in the last line - all conspire to muddy both
the picture and the heartfelt message.

I've no doubt there was something to be said here. It was said but the picture seems undeveloped. A few more seconds in the processing vat would likely bring out a more favorable contrast so that we may better see the beautiful outlines and contours of shading, the subtle nuance of emotion that it yearns so desperately to portray.

Redeeming Features

Many days... yes, sometimes the ideas do not wish to be written down. They just float about in our minds and refuse to congregate into anything worthy of sharing. Who knows the reasons? They are many, no doubt and unique to each person. Failure to sleep is a different problem but again with potentially many reasons. This poem certainly points out those facts in a succinct but rather choppy and terse fashion. I doubt it will thrill most English readers but I could be wrong. However it does communicate clearly and that's probably its most redeeming feature. Keep at it.

Arguable Successes

I think this piece falls under the poetry-as-a-catchall category. While I believe that I understand free verse, as a form of poetry, for me, these words are more of a philosophical (very) short story; maybe even a parable of sorts. It is delightful and there is little to disagree with in the thesis. However, I wonder if perhaps, with a bit more thought, one might include additional aspects or interpretations regarding the meaning of life. But, as has been mentioned, its success lies mostly in its simplicity and who can argue with success?

Timeless Idiots

TIME... One summer, I removed my wristwatch and did not put it back on until the following summer. I was aware of its absence at the oddest moments. I now wonder why I did it. Perhaps I thought that by discarding the most obvious keeper of time I could, myself, step outside of it. It was an idiot's thought and it was then that I became determined to pursue life as though I was indeed an idiot. I ask you now, quite plainly, have I or have I not succeeded?

Natural Whims

Imagine a conveyance that, as the eye beholds it from the aft as a rustic oxcart and then, proceeding along its length to fore, melds into a Rolls ornamented hood. I gasp at the creation as it roars, creaks, squeaks and ambles along in a profusion of protrusions; much like a many-legged centipede searching its way through that forest's undergrowth. What, on the earth or in the earth, is it searching for? It does seem a bit absurd to see it crawl over this an that, hell-bent upon a destination at which we may only guess. The only thing we know for sure is that it is there and it is in motion. The rest is, if I may twist your eloquence slightly, a beauty typical of ones natural whims.

Embellished Rooms

I presume that you, like I, trust in the annals of history. But how much of any person that becomes legend is fact versus the buttressing and adornment of the poet? Should we, the reader, give more weight to fact or demur to the thrill of the embellished storied? Perhaps, with understanding, there is room for both.

Ill Pills

Since you have given us few hints then it may/must be (as in the title) that we are free to choose; it is a question of choice. Do I choose to see the spikes upright, menacing or perhaps there is some leeway and they're lying flat, in a box or boxed in a flat.

The material of those spikes may be relevant as well. Are they steel, wood, something hard and durable or perhaps spikes of young, tender grass or young seedling trees; freshly sprouted and seeking the sky? Far off is relative, isn't it? When something catches the eye distance is measured in terms of focus and objective. What is the objective here? Perhaps to challenge the reader to look at things afresh, from a different perspective?

If they will "never sway, wind blown" then we can probably rule out the organic, the living. Hold on... "while I stay away?" Hmm... so they could become wind-blown if you DON'T stay away? As the robot in my head is won't to say, "DOES NOT COMPUTE." So, true my dear, imaginary robotic voice-in-my-head; and then we have to wonder if an affect can really be effective? Curious.

But wait. Now we have a gauge to measure relative. The bridge... is it of human, industrial or epic/legendary proportions. Thrown over we are, down onto the needle point of this missive. There I lay, impaled upon the spikes, bleeding out a pool of gory demise, questioning my choices of literal or metaphor, innuendo or allegory. Where did I put that chill-pill? I feel ill.

Chapter 23

Salmon Footprints

There is an echo and a disconnect. The echo is both visual and sonic made manifest by the end repetitions in the two stanzas. It entices the reader to stand upon a ragged cliff that overlooks a wilderness of metaphors that seek an outward nature to compare and contrast with a savaged human interior. An interior crafted by a somber and reflective architect that has just paid the outrageous interest on overdue love. Now, bereft of legal tender, the dead salmon poses nature's allegorical question... in the night, we see the candle, the pillow, and the dust behind the locked door but whose footprints are these?

Continuing Lessons

I have read, in various places, writers that compare time to a river or a stream; something flowing. Occasionally, there is a reference to the beginning or the end of time. It is compared to sunrise and sunset, birth and death... but always flowing. In truth, it is not that way here in this invocation. Here, time presents itself as a moment; a hard-rock candy that, melting slowly upon the tongue, flavors life and being with a gentle, mournful call for companionship. A heart bared in yearning for one that can share a view of eternity that is at once both blissful and frames prayer as recognition of the unknown and unknowable. If time could speak, what might it say? Could it explain to one caught so fully in it's grasp the true nature of immortality? What words could it use that might lift a silent soulful voice toward a heaven'd sky; where longing and loneliness have no place in the lexicon of that existence? The questions remain. The lessons continue... abide with me.

Universal Truths

At the Universal Philosophers Comedy Club (members only) no crying is allowed. There are no comedians; only the audience/members. At random someone will take the stage, pick up the microphone and state what they believe to be a "universal truth." After which everyone (usually) laughs riotously and takes a drink. Sarcasm is optional. There is no shortage of material... ever. Oddly enough everyone seems to leave satisfied.

Espresso Brains

This is a strange and delightful change of focus. I've never read the "warring seasons" expressed in quite this manner. To me it is very similar to the abstract and impressionist schools warring against each other as they struggle for dominance between an older, gentler dialect and that of the newer, abrasive style of modernism. For all its complexity it is eminently readable; something that is often a challenge with your work. But this one appeals to the intellectual croissant with morning stimulant indulgence side of my brain. If this is a free sample then I'll take a dozen more with an espresso, please.

Pickup Sticks

This piece is like my pittance, spent to rent tillage in the fall then going into the field on the first fine spring day and seeing it infested with Beatles and Stones and then trying to explain to them that they ought not be there and they yammers back at me but I can't understand a word they're saying. Where upon I sit down on that winter-bludgeoned soil and dream of a life of luxury that'll never be. Such a choice you have, XY. Pick up sticks or buy me a pint. What's your pleasure?

Tempting Fruit

I think I must like the way you jiggle the line (or something), you know, this style of titled fishing? I'm a bit chagrined that I always seem to take the bait and, good grief, I can't believe I'm saying this... actually enjoy biting and chewing on these barbed hooks of yours as I thrash about, breaching the surface and splashing back under, gasping for Ginger to fulfill Gilligan's incessant fantasy. Good god, my lips are sore. Got any lemonade? I need a bit more painful pucker; around the edges, just there... kiss me sweet, you tempting fruit.

Careless Considerations

Artistic, literary and with a touch of tantalizing philosophical indulgence. A striking, school-spanning canvas of words. Rather like an Charles River or impressionist piece cum Frieda Khalo. Well done, XX. This one made me think too! ...just talking to myself here understand: There is no doubt that the words of the poet can and do transcend the boundaries between worlds (real, imaginary or both). That transcendence is the journey. The destination or goal however is quite another matter. If a poet should dare to thrust their pen toward the heavens then they should also be prepared for the consequences. What is immortality that mere mortals should seek it so? Perhaps we should have a care in this regard lest we find our souls entwined in eternity, not with perfect love but with endless reflections of self-adoration. Forever is a long time to ponder the outcome of careless consideration.

Spilling Heads

I must say that I have recently wanted to do this. To close my eyes and type in the dark. Sadly, I discovered that I need to figure out a way to keep a blank page in this computer typewriter without turning on the page lights. It a challenge! I love this piece. I can't say why exactly. Perhaps it's just the implicit overlap of ideas or the common familiarity of the phrasing of those candid ideas. Personally, I think you should try this more often... try sitting in the dark, large sheet of paper, and just upon waking in the morning... write what you see/hear/feel/think/experience. I would be most interested to read what spills out of your head at that time!

Endless Possibilities

I make a distinction here, with this piece, between what we are taught as children and what we come to learn as adults. As children we are (usually) praised when it seems our lessons are learned correctly and (more often) admonished when they reflect distorted. However, as adults these lessons, these words especially, come to have new meaning and the foundations built during youth often crumble in places. To sacrifice, to serve, remaining steadfast or to quietly wander away. These choices seem intended for only those minds that have reached a certain level of promiscuity with the ways of the world. There are opportunities and opportunists; both a necessary contrivance of destiny's call and, as always, the possibilities are endless.

Warning Labels

#35 is still alive; my how you thrive! A feast for soul cannibals and love butchers! The counterpoint of lunge, parry, thrust, slice, dice... mighty nice, used thrice to entice those poor lice that feed in the bleeding follicles caused by self-inflicted scratching. XX, every one of your pieces should come with a mandatory warning label; much like all costly pharma. Perhaps something simple though and to the point? "WARNING: Contents may cure you if it doesn't kill you first."

Chapter 24

Brave Pens

What would you have me say to this? Should I comment on the selection and placement of this dust of Cantor? Perhaps on the serious levity of its packaging? Or maybe just a pat on the back and an acknowledgment of the skill and bravery required to pen this... especially the bravery.

Knuckle Writers

I put on my shark-mind and since then my teeth always renew so this didn't affect me one little bit. Nope, it wasn't like fingernails on the chalkboard or that whine of the drill or my knuckles turning white as they grip the firmament of leather bound steel. None of that could surface through the memory of scenes from The Marathon Man. Do me a favor XY. Next time write a little less artistically, OK? ☻

Balloon Senses

Finally, you've found a voice and something worth writing about. No, not the message that you're giving up but rather the way that you said it. The clarity and tone. That was original. Only you could say it just that way and have it make sense... and with a sure and resolute emphasis that encourages us to suspend disbelief. But, really, how could you quit writing?! You're a writer, aren't you?.

I see others have tried to change your mind. Still others have decided to wish you well on your way to where ever not-writing takes you. I'll bet you're curious (you're still reading, aren't you?) at which way I'm going to flop... how is Caesar's thumb pointing? Does thumbs up mean live or die? I could never remember. But, I digress.

Writing can be fun and to some it can be an addiction. Ambition, that sense of ego and accomplishment and desire for the admiration of others... it is all good and well but it shouldn't get in the way of the need to fulfill a desire for expressing ones self in writing. Or for asking people to read what you've written for that matter.

However, putting your work out there for everyone to criticize is not always (fun). Sometimes people tell you what they think and let's be honest; not everything that people write is fit to print. Some of it isn't even fit to read. As in the movie "Dirty Harry" and the oft quoted line, "A man's (woman, thing) got to know his/her/its limitations."

But since you're a fan of skiing here's a skiing analogy... you don't quit skiing just because someone says "you suck", rather you quit (if you quit) because it's just not worth the trouble. There is no more joy to be found in the activity or you find that you'll not be able to pay the rent doing it. How sad. I didn't win a medal in the Olympics so I'm just going to quit skiing altogether. How stupid is that? It's like saying I'm never going to love or be loved again because I'm not good at it.

Now, see what you've done? You've forced me to write something that might be considered rude and/or offensive. I had to, you know, it felt good too. Because everything I write is practically perfect in every way. (Yes, it was stolen from me and put into that movie, Mary Poppins.) I'm kidding, of course.

OK, here's my opinion on your well-written missive. Do what you will. If you want to give up then nothing anyone can say will probably change that. If you want to keep writing then do that. Again, I doubt anyone can change your mind once it's made a decision. I say that because of the strength of this obituary-like piece. If you are determined to commit artistic suicide than by all means do what you must. On the other hand, if you should come to your senses and decide to prick that balloon of an ego that swells between your competent ears then you may find not just a few that will welcome you back to your senses; perhaps with a sheepish grin on your face but a welcome none the less.

Transcending Imitation

I think/hope it's enough that we acknowledge your humanity; you certainly have here. The words can help but perhaps it is what remains unwritten, unspoken, intimated that transcends.

Fishy Words

I like this one! ...je ne sais quoi... For all of those reasons that would probably seem so ho-hum. We live in a sea of words... and yet, sometimes it's hard to fish out just the right ones to make that special comment for someone you've come to admire and care about. ("Now, don't go get'n mushy on me," she says.)

Tide Sweepings

I sat on the beach and spoke these words into the sunset and surf. It didn't help. The tide came in and I was... swept away.

Sustaining Morsels

Deaf, dumb and blind I walk into this motorcade of words. But there are no accolades for me only a good man-gling if I'm unlucky. Perhaps a quick death if I am. While it is possible to knit a thing that resembles a sweater from paper graffiti, it's longevity and serviceability will surely be a topic for discussion at some point. Better I think to plow your own fields and harvest from a garden closer to your true nature. But that is not to say that travel will not be beneficial. Just remember to bring a change of scenery with you and a few morsels to sustain your appetite.

Strange Poetry

Random you say? Thoughts? I think it's quite mysterious. I mean, why else would you just randomly start writing something dark and then, as though on a whim, choose
certain key words to emphasize with color? A psych or, better yet, a psi-op would look beyond the poem. To them this
would be a remote view through your mind to an unknown
force, a point or points of origin that use this highway of
thought and imagination that you have so willingly provided. But, and this is the mystery, if you are the highway
then what or who is the destination? Which reader will
read and be transformed; perhaps unknowingly? See, what
happens, when you write strange poetry? {goose bumps}
☺

Twisted Lists

The ladies of the Royal Riddling Sorority After consult-
ing with many authorities Suggest that when making a
list as twisted as this It's really best to ensure none are
priorities.

Idiot Riddles

Why is it that obscure writing ever becomes the heir
apparent to the most exquisitely sharpened contrasts?
Rhetorically, I suggest it is because of the talent for walking in ever larger circles of perspicuity. He can do no wrong
that writes riddles for idiots. But, there is a warm place
in our hearts for all fools that warm themselves by setting

their clothes ablaze and at the last moment dousing the danger with the tankard of ale remaining in their other hand; before it can more fully illuminate that dire situation.

Sleeping Words

Somewhere, perhaps in a distant future time, someone finds a dusty bottle; a curl of yellowed paper within. Fishing it out they read these words. Our XY is long since dust but these... these memories, these words are forever and "... words never sleep."

Chapter 25

Chunking Times

I'm just not inclined to pick this apart too much because I really enjoyed the reading of it. I could easily relate to it. Possibly because it reminds me of those years when I lived among the giant redwoods of the California coast near Santa Cruz. There, at this time of year one may look out over the ocean from a mountain top, just near the end of day, and see the sun "swing on beams of dusk." Or, in this case perhaps, see it as both sunset and sunrise; those "...days that are still unborn."

The reader's mind... a curious and a never-ending source of fascination. For example, Gerald and I are reversed on the first line. It took me several reads to accept the unusual allegory but the use of 'remind' didn't bother me at all. The 'gliding' along the rivers edge had me going though as I kept trying to visualize how you might do this and still experience the skimming, gripping, and releasing; what mode of movement or conveyance would be appropriate? Running barefoot, riding a bicycle, or perhaps just floating in the mind's eye and mixing memories in a synesthesiastic montage?

The "non-linear path" of life actually reminded me of a thesis I read a long time ago. It was an experiment that used a very high-speed camera and flash in order capture a photograph of a bullet striking a metal washer edge-on. The washer can be seen clearly moving from it's initial starting position to a position a few centimeters downrange and still well within the view of the camera. The odd thing is that the arc of the washers travel, seen in the photograph as a steak of reflected light, simply disappears for a small part of the arc-of-travel and then reappears a bit later. The unique conclusion of this was that time is NOT LINEAR but occurs in discrete chunks. One chunk of time begins where another ends; almost. The interval between these "chunks" of time, while very small, was measurable and the gap in the washer's arc of travel supposedly proved this. It was repeatable and, according to the author, not an anomaly of the equipment, the setup or the execution of the experiment. So... perhaps there really are "...spaces between" where only you can see and life may not be entirely linear after all. {thunk, thunk}

The last stanza is a nice one to think of as I drift off to sleep.

Crib Notes

>Q-Q< I wonder, in a former life, did you perhaps own a motorcycle and some dark sunglasses? There should be.. no, scratch that.. Q-tilde-aside - I hear bongos in that waltz, somewhere; and perhaps the rhythmic snapping of fingers amidst the aroma of unfiltered cigarettes and goth-drab double espressos. Then, there's you, under a tiny spot, sitting on a stool on a riser'd stage with a cameo moon backdrop that slowly fades in and out to the cycles of a rotating multi-gel-filtered back light.

This one is a rather strange read for me. But hey, it's

you. I've gotten so used to being able to peek under the covers that it seems strange when you put one out there without any crib notes.

Gaah! I don't know. I'm under water on this one, XY. {glub, glug}

Speaking Cats

You speak the nature of the cat that speaks the nature of the existential human. It's strangely satisfying. I read. I am happy. What more could you want?

Swirling Lights

I had the thought to print this upon thin, translucent paper... then cut the lines into strips and affix them, in their proper order, skewed as a slowly descending spiral upon a small, golden-amber rotating lampshade. Positioned beside a bed or perhaps a cozy reading spot it would surely provide a languid sea of swirling light and shadow; a warm reminder that the hurt, the loneliness and gloom of an otherwise drab existence can be held at bay with only a few well-chosen words. Sensuous, warm, endearing... simply marvelous.

Quiet Mournings

You've probably never heard of a director by the name of Silvio Soldino. He directed an Italian movie, "Bread & Tulips", the description: "...a gentle comedy about a housewife who temporarily flees from the grinding tedium of her household duties and drifts into a world of amicable weirdos." Lucia Maglienta, as the housewife, brings the same sense of melancholy (not depression) to the screen as you do to this piece. I like to think that we, as authors, have some smidgen of say in the final draft of our lives; perhaps not, but it's a naiveté that I permit myself.

As you draw upon the ever-growing depths of your experience never fear the edits and rewrites. You, of all people, should know this best having both the pleasure and the pain of being your own harshest critic in such matters. Still, all of that aside, it does not detract one iota from the popcorn tear-jerker that you have offered up here. It's like trying to stare into the eyes of one of those sad little puppies that often accompany the leash of life so unwillingly.

It's probably a good thing that there is a vast physical distance separating us otherwise I should be compelled to seek you out upon discovering that you've had one of those "quiet mournings" and offer to ply you with fresh coffee, tasty nibbles and some cheerful conversation.

Different Ways

It's a good poem. It says what it is meant to say. Still, the camaraderie, the human aspect of killing; these things always seem more personal. Yet in truth, not a day goes by that a we live only because something else dies. It's like there is this balance to the universe that must be maintained at all cost. If so, it begs the question of how the value of one life can differ from another. Everyone answers that question for themselves, eventually, in their own way.

Silver Bells

It's good enough. Both beautiful and brilliant too. Also, there is a sense of practical magic to this but without the intent of warding off disaster by invoking the seemingly impossible. For in this, the impossible is desired, the probable is seen through the wrong end of the telescope; distant, yet approachable by this offering of the soul and of the heart that desires an affinity of close coupling in all possible imaginings. The curious hungry bees see your bloom unfolding, XX. Do you hear them buzzing round you in your garden of verse? Do you see the glint of their wings in the sunlight? Ring the little silver bell with ardor and let the days begin anew; each and every one.

Unnecessary Surfaces

When does the infatuation with words end? Will that time ever be for you or me? I try to imagine thinking without having ever learned a verbal/spoken language; what must that be like? Is it even possible? Hmm, sure it is. Helen Keller - trapped in her own head until... great story. It saddens me to think that the pages (work, I presume) whittles you down. Even if you enjoy something eventually it can become an stimulus of ignoration (yep, just made that one up, don't bother looking for it). So, let's have that Johnny Depp dream, the one where the ship sails upside down on the membrane between ocean and air. Swimming to the surface should then become unnecessary. Eh, wot? ☺

Sentimental Pluckings

Please, add me to your list of admirers on this one. Done in a 'midnight huff', eh? Well, so be it. It's kind of you to open up, as it were. Perhaps you are shy, if one were to meet you in person; and yet there is a firmness to these words that might seem at odds with your self-representation of the cafe-cornered observer, poking about on a laptop, sipping a latte (or whatever.) This one has an erratic attraction that binds the mind to the expansive lexicon invoked on behalf of self and prospective observers that would dissect and catalog the lines in order to better understand, to know, and perhaps to determine if there is a kinship to be had from their understanding. If the shore appears muddy then I contend it may only be the angle of an obtuse reflection. One that, as it changes, will reveal the shore with a brighter clarity as the arc of your life climbs higher toward zenith. Oh, don't worry... we, your readers, will be delighted to do as much of that sentimental plucking as you may be willing to permit.

Word States

"B**R! Helping Ugly People Have S*x Since 1862." I prefer soft-baked chocolate almond oatmeal cookies myself. ☺ ... If it's hot when I have a garage sale then I like to sit somewhere in the shade. Usually someone will come along and sit down beside me and begin to chit-chat, sometimes about the price of stuff. Stuff I used to care about, perhaps a lot, but has now lost some of its relevance; more so with the passage of time. ... So, what your really saying is... the problem is not how to be single. The problem is what to do when the world doesn't meet expectations. The problem is what to do when love is not enough. The problem is how one (alone) should think about the world when something reaches inside and pulls out a chunk of our heart and starts to nibble on it while we consider watching that surreal movie play over and over and over again in our head... for a time longer than infinity plus one.

"...UN-matrimonied." Love it! It's seems a unique way of labeling a wasteland scenario with an indeterminate half-life where the fallout and emotional radiation tends to mutate all things within its proximity using the inverse-square-law. Acquaintances develop rashes and close friends sometimes mutate into three-eyed thick-lipped gnostics. The outlines of once solid community and family recede into an ever-dimming gray fog bank of historical contexts that offer buffets of condolence, well-meaning sympathies and cheery hope-covered nuggets of righteous moral fortitude.

Perhaps it is the case that being "single" is an illusion or a state of learned-indifference, a small deceit that some part of our heart and mind plays upon that which remains. The aftershock from the resulting UN-matrimony an attempt to pull apart, to subdivide the continents of self leaving only a fragile isthmus connecting all those destinations we believed to be so important. Unacceptable. No. As long as there is breath and a heartbeat it can never be that.

Single... singular or a plurality of cosmic singularities; these are mighty and fundamental concepts but flawed by indelible, unfathomable ignorance. Let us rejoice as best we can in that ignorance for it gives a truer sense of purpose in the knowing that we have only just begun to explore the possibilities of the word-state.

The Ages

Perhaps it's all about watching the snow melt and being aware of what's going on around during that time... being aware of life. But when it's nearing the end then enough with the joy and the suffering; let it be done with. On the last day, perhaps metaphorically the last day of life, all those times of life-play are lost to the ages and melt away.

Perfect Circles

A girl, crouching/sitting on a bronze beach... curly hair, like seaweed, tumbling over her back and shoulders. Hands circle the face while elbows jut forward over the knees as she gazes into the distant ocean horizon. I hear it, see it, smell it, feel it. I'm curious as to what she's thinking, if anything. Perhaps she's achieved a state of no-mind and has become the rocks, the seaweed, the apple of life or perhaps the perfect circle.

Angry Flowers

Every visitor needs a map and the notes are welcome. But that doesn't stop the random tourist from transmogrifying reality to suit themselves. It's not a statue with pigeon poop on it; it's a work of art. Let the transmogrification begin... from office to rink.

So, again we see... as you've implied before, you don't always keep your eye on the puck while the game is in progress, do you? Sometimes you daydream... those curious little twisted beasties that we've all come to know and love. The ones that make you a U-U (wuz gonna say yo-yo but it sounds like I be rapp'n, dog, ya know?) on a string of up and down merry-go-round cardboard cutout carousel figures. We hear the music of the Calliope and are drawn to the garish primary colors that, at once, both illuminate and silhouette the riders as it diverts attentions and masks the the interior motor; the mind that is you my dear XY.

I wonder, if you carve little animals out of soap and use them in the shower, will it imbue one with the characteristics of the carved effigy? ~ Bob, the Angry Flower[1].

---

1. www.angryflower.com

Chapter 26

Invisible Spectrums

They didn't get it. Hell, I don't get it... but I want too. There's something there too. Something important... something that should be comprehended, understood, assimilated, cherished. But what is it? It's driving me crazy... it seems there, just out of reach and each time I read it there is a slight trip-up-down, a stumble and a fall, from grace perhaps or other - hard to tell; it's illusive. And that is the joy and wonder of it all, isn't it? It begs us to ignore the scaffolding of rhyme that ornaments this ancient message woven into the fabric of unconscious knowing. Ignore the asymmetry of forms and embrace the irregular contours of thought that overlay and plumb true the mind's horizon lines. What have you done? What have you wrought that sparkles in the invisible spectrum of almost-there? All I ask is just this... keep writing. Maybe, someday, I'll get it. I certainly hope to.

Solemn Retreats

Sometimes, I just get lucky. I think this might be one of those times. What I get from this piece is nothing less than a sense of deft, atonal rapture. There are lyrical notes emerging from beneath the gray overlay that keep just ahead of the mind's eye at a wheel-turning pace via tempos of prosaic color opposites. I wonder, randomly, if the the use of cyan with the word "red" has further enhanced the dextro-levorotory sensations of balanced dizziness that each unseparated stanza tattoo upon themselves with hidden perforations; made with the rounded tip of the phrasing palette knife. I've read similar things, snippets of Whitman and others... and this too has a sense of deep sensory cultivation and respect for observation that bears itself out in the balanced calculus of the hidden forms. A superior work that should be read by more, many more... and in the best times and traditions of solemn retreat.

Diversionary Plaster

The orbit of this one is surely elliptical for there is a special spot; the foci at each end that resonates. It starts with a querulous whisper at one (the beginning) and is inevitably focused by those carefully curved walls of smooth, diversionary plaster until they conjoin and evolve into a exclamatory mental-infinity at the other (the end) and emerge both magnified and splashed with emotional color. A marvelous construction.

Deviating Revisions

Well, this is passing strange. An eyelash fluttering in a dream, overtaken by the displacement of senses that seem translated into dimensions illuminated by the choice of random questions related to a self-cognizant world-view morphology. I haven't a clue where you're going with this but it is pretty. Rather like coming upon a patch of wild-flowers within a sunny clearing in a thick forest. I like the natural allusions bound to the transmuted eternal questions of existence. They lend a sort of credibility to the whole thing that might otherwise require a bit more structure for proper assimilation. The assumptions are hopeful if a bit childlike. There are few self-aware seers; only self-proclaimed and they often do not bear up under time-bound factoring. The thing that throws me for a loop though is the word "barracks." For me, it stands out like a pylon jutting up from the sand of an otherwise pristine beach. It plumbs my fathomed depths as to the price of it's unobvious purchase. Well, it's a wonderful draft. I am most curious to see how any revision may deviate.

Existential Corners

This begs a reference; both before and after reading. Of course you, XY, have provided that in the notes. But the reference I refer to is not one from books, or movies, or even conversation. It is a deeper, darker reference that can only be extracted from that place within each reader where such things exist that are paid for with tokens of unspeakable contemplations. Within these thought-shadows, voices beckon to 'mortal men of moment', sketched so casually in this piece but with a subtle force, evident by the deep creases left upon the reader's mind. I fear your entanglement with this poorly lit corner of existence is far from over. Perhaps never.

Carnal Intellects

The analogy... women and horses... will suffer one another until each species, in it's own turn, departs into many-layered time. As this piece evokes, I can but wonder who would wager on the winner of that race. Of the two, all men know that the woman would be the more offended if the wager should both be and not be placed. It is this primal confusion, this opposition of willing want versus desire that most differentiates the two and yet the love for the former can not exist without a studied comparison to the latter. Perhaps we should simply sigh, admire those "meadow-sweet grass ... formed ... flanks..." and leave the mysteries of their origin to the more curious and less carnal intellect.

Hello Smiles

I've had the grave dream before too. It was mostly as you describe but you omitted the part about the passage of time, the rotting of the wood, the burrowing of the earthworms, the roots coming down from the flowers growing above and then traveling upward through these into the brilliant light of day as a floating, joyous orb of spirit. I hope you have this version if there is ever a next time.

Time to come out of the shadows and say hello to the light and smile. Here, let's practice... put your fingers on each side of your mouth and push, upwards. There ya go!! ☻ {pats forehead and smiles}

Some Days

The "little death", tugging where ever it can get some traction. ...a merry-go-round, broken down. "I'll fix it soon." ... sure you will and some day I'll know what love is.

Strange Flourishing

Ah... expedition destination reservation commiseration elucidation fornication in negation. It's who/where we all are at times. Yes indeed. Strangely flourished too I might add but palatable none the less.

Possible Lips

The water seeks the container... a glass worthy of holding its essence just that close but open to the lips of possibility.

Kneaded Compliments

I started at the end, then the beginning. Now, walking toward the middle... no, not this piece; though it, by itself, is telling. No, I'm talking about the collection of "you." All of this. It goes without saying that you have found an articulation for the more pressed and delineated abstractions of the mind. I'm pretty sure I'm going to have a vivid response to almost everything that you have or will write. How's that for a compliment? Like you needed one, right? ☺

Chapter 27

Fluid Definitions

It has that excellent active-interruption between each stanza of distilled, condensed contemplative emotion. I think that is what makes it stand out; unique among many other things that lay bleeding and wounded upon the backdrop of life. It's a keen image of self that seems a reflection from a finely polished blade. One that has been sharpened by the rigors of unwanted experience and a resolute quest for absolution.

At your request... personally, speaking only in terms that have fluid definitions, as something to read, I judge it worthy. You may find some respite, some diversion/solace around here, Captain. Welcome... and thank you.

Blooming Flowers

Sometimes we get so wrapped up in the day-to-day, the eking part, that we loose sight of what was once our reason for being. Sadly, some may never have gotten even that far. It is for those that we should at least feign some small token of pity. Or perhaps some real honest-to-God pity... for all concerned. But, what good is pity? It doesn't really do much in the long run, does it? It's just a reaction to a condition that seems out of control... one that needs some tears of pity to lubricate that reliable clockwork of self-denial of all things important and holy. Those last three stanzas redeem us. The clock isn't broken after all. It just needs to be reset. There we are... good as new, right as rain on a dry day. Maybe those flowers will bloom yet. What do you think?

Better Things

You've cut me deep. I'm not here to judge. That's not my purpose this time around. I'm here... to be redundant, to point out the obvious, to make lite of the serious and frown upon the lack of compassion that must yet still exist. Perhaps it is a bit of all of this that keeps "us" in those dark places, in those shadows where our hearts, our souls shrivel and die or at least seem to. Are the heart and soul connected? I don't know. They're both as abstract at times as those thrown daggers and shrapnel spray are real. The one thing we can take away from this with any certainty is that we do not, cannot know the purpose, if such exists, for these events that riddle our lives with incomprehensible dichotomies. Hate, sorrow, remorse... affirmation, hope, love. It's a delicate balance of interaction, of understanding, of assimilation. We experience; hopefully we learn and grow just enough to move on to something better... for everyone.

Limitless Oceans

I compare the beginning with the middle and the end, I guess. You do a lot of screaming in this piece but, you know, I just didn't feel someone really, truly screaming. Instead I saw someone waving a flag, as though from a mountain top in the distance; through some sort of bluish haze. Something like that. Here's why. It's all about the end words in the stanzas; the rushing waters, the endless skies, the immortal earth... and those raging fires. But those fires are not about consumption or decimation or conflagration. No. They're about fires of passion... pent up in a prison of frustration. It's the primal cause for the 'crimson prayers'. Again, the crimson isn't so much about the color or the heat of a fire as it is about the determination and will to bloom... to seek a means to represent the light of inspiration and observation that burns so brightly. I'm glad you added the author's note. It clarifies and confirms the determination of this latent spell: earth, sky, water, fire and the crimson passion offered up in supplication to any with eyes to see, ears to hear, mind to think and heart to feel.

What an excellent springboard it makes to jump into that limitless ocean that is you.

Real Fantasies

Of course you know that this is an incredibly desperate tone, don't you? The problem for a reader is to discern if art and reality have become blended into this canvas of words in such a way that they might act upon this plea for a Dudley Doright to come to the aid of L'll Nell that has been tied to the railroad tracks by the evil Snidely Whiplash. Do I call the mounties out and try to save poor Nell or do I think of wine & cheese in the gallery of despair and admire the canvas that keeps me guessing about the light that was used to render the reader dazed and confused as to the reality of the drama depicted in this scene? So, on a scale of one to ten - ten being absolute fantasy - where is this piece?

Individual Equals

This is idealism. In actuality, individual equality is an illusion of idealism. An individual within a society is very much like an element within an algebraic equation; metaphorically speaking. It is the mix of operators, variables, values and constants on both sides of an equation that, when solving for a particular variable (person) make it (them) equal... just as a society both defines and instantiates the concept of 'equality' for an individual within that society.

Mind Killers

I've heard it said that the choices we make in life are things we agreed to do before we were born. Because we had something to learn. I don't know if it's true or not. It's just another one of those things that seems to offer a bit of temporary solace and a shelter from the embarrassment at having made such poor decisions. Fear and doubt; the mind killers and guilt the destroyer of souls.

Stripey Pants

The most coherent and entertaining babble I have read in quite some time. Close rhyming with fish hooks of un-restrained demarcation; rather like tilling the garden with dynamite and planting with a shotgun. Now, that probably doesn't give you much of a clue but my smile is equal to the that of the cat and shall surely stay that way for some time to come. But, I confess, I had to rest... for the length and breadth of this great expanse could tax a repelephant in stripy pants.

Soup Labels

Mouth closed, a sound issues forth from my nostrils... "hummph." There is no indication of direction. A mote floats in the silence of an afternoon sunbeam. A goat stands, chewing on my old shoe. Where is my guilt for not having provided better fare?

Faithful Feelings

Do we choose the words or do the words choose us? Vessels of thought, emotion and subject to the whims of those "peevish beasts." It is the nature of failure that defines the word itself as it cannot and does not fully achieve anything close to an embodiment, so personal, so unbalanced - and as you say it twirls and turns and wreaks havoc upon the spirit that it seeks to encompass. These dark shadows, these inky ethereal forms ... they seek out, they envy, they lust - it is their nature, their need, their hunger - insatiable it would seem. But, a sense of self and faith in something, anything really, will cause them to retreat.

Chapter 28

Pensive Inkdrops

I can only wonder at what brought this into being. Yes, I read the cliff notes earlier, around the cuff of your sleeve, but it has me somewhat puzzled as to why it takes the form of an adulterated (and I use that term loosely) prayer for children at bedtime?

There is an earthy tone that permeates you; your words. It is rich and fertile in a way that encourages verdant thoughts to bloom with anticipation of what may soon be, in its time, Spring. But for now there is the warmth and coziness of double/triple entendre quits. I come back to your diner because the menu is almost always worth the extra travel. Plus, the bottomless coffee cup.

Padded Paws

The allegorical is often illusive for a reader. Here there
is no mental Mississippi to float down at a leisurely pace,
where one may take comfort in the fact that firmament
bounds the flow of thoughts. As with the terminus at the
mouth of a gulf.. a life too can meander in its search for
places to nestle, to find that warmth of light that seems so
often to provide an attractive contrast to an otherwise dark
and turbulent flow. There is the subtle inorganic mixed in
with the predominately organic tone that seems to provide a necessary contrast in this otherwise subtle and soft-
walking caricature.

Sparkling Gems

One hundred years ago a fountain pen was invented with
a special feature. It had a half moon shaped curve of metal
that protruded from its side - like one arm akimbo. It is
said that this feature alone set it apart from all others
because when it was lain upon a table it could not roll
off onto the floor. For this it was said to be a "profanity
saver." In this your arm is akimbo and it cannot roll to an
undesired place. It too is a profanity saver.

Slaving Scribes

Well now, there is the toil of minions applied to a questionable project of potentially epic proportions... transmogrify the English language into something that is both phonetic when spoken and symbolic when written. I await your blueprints for this dreadnought of linguistics.

Indifferent Pools

I don't know what it is but I like it; especially the bloated, angry frogs.

Pearl Earrings

In every age there is a mechanic determinism that imposes itself upon the art and artist that abides in that sliver of time. It is as though lesser Vermeers have rallied in support of guilders and in so doing have provided bread to the sellers of minerals and oil - the ingredients that grind true art into a framed submission. Every painting has its flaws otherwise it would not be human. This is very human.

Constant Changes

Friends... they make us happy, they make us sad. Life seeks balance, always and change is the only constant. Everything has its limits; everything can "break." Even friends. Beyond life, who knows? Perhaps the rules change then. Perhaps.

Golden Threads

Layers of words cannot occlude what was meant to be
revealed. Attraction, repulsion... goal-seeking revulsion; all
of this and more are in the deck from which our cards
are dealt. As this makes perfectly clear that treasure is
a word of many meanings. What we value in life reveals
much about our values and our worth to others and to the
world in which we exist. If they have mass then weight is
implicit when other bodies come near. Let's hope the orbits
are elliptical or perhaps a near miss. Collisions should be
avoided if at all possible.

Harmon Kardons

Message: IF "grasp at redemption" AND "forgive and
give what is good" THEN "karma harmonized."
Does this apply to people that are "practically perfect in
every way?" Just curious. Is it not-good to be of good cheer
when someone else is trying to be serious? Or is it just bad
manners? Not polite? Uncivilized? Curious those things
that make one feel "guilty" and seek "redemption", isn't it?
Some more weighty than others but by what standards and
why the need to grade them into levels in the first place?
There is only one punishment for life... death. Everything
else is just in between. There, see... now you've done it
again with those gosh-darn thingamabobs of yours.

Eking Pity

Sometimes we get so wrapped up in the day-to-day, the eking part, that we loose sight of what was once our reason for being. Sadly, some may never have gotten even that far. It is for those that we should at least feign some small token of pity. Or perhaps some real honest-to-God pity... for all concerned. But, what good is pity? It doesn't really do much in the long run, does it? It's just a reaction to a condition that seems out of control... one that needs some tears of pity to lubricate that reliable clockwork of self-denial of all things important and holy. Those last three stanzas redeem us. The clock isn't broken after all. It just needs to be reset. There we are... good as new, right as rain on a dry day. Maybe those flowers will bloom yet. What do you think?

Chapter 29

Redundant Darkness

X, you've cut me deep. I'm not here to judge. That's not my purpose this time around. I'm here... to be redundant, to point out the obvious, to make lite of the serious and frown upon the lack of compassion that must yet still exist. Perhaps it is a bit of all of this that keeps "us" in those dark places, in those shadows where our hearts, our souls shrivel and die or at least seem to. Are the heart and soul connected? I don't know. They're both as abstract at times as those thrown daggers and shrapnel spray are real. The one thing we can take away from this with any certainty is that we do not, cannot know the purpose, if such exists, for these events that riddle our lives with incomprehensible dichotomies. Hate, sorrow, remorse... affirmation, hope, love. It's a delicate balance of interaction, of understanding, of assimilation. We experience; hopefully we learn and grow just enough to move on to something better... for everyone.

Ocean You

You're probably wondering why I'm looking at your oldest/first posting here. I'm not sure why I do it either; just curious as I compare the beginning with the middle and the end, I guess. You do a lot of screaming in this piece but, you know, I just didn't feel someone really, truly screaming. Instead I saw someone waving a flag, as though from a mountain top in the distance; through some sort of bluish haze. Something like that. Here's why. It's all about the end words in the stanzas; the rushing waters, the endless skies, the immortal earth... and those raging fires. But those fires are not about consumption or decimation or conflagration. No. They're about fires of passion... pent up in a prison of frustration. It's the primal cause for the 'crimson prayers'. Again, the crimson isn't so much about the color or the heat of a fire as it is about the determination and will to bloom... to seek a means to represent the light of inspiration and observation that burns so brightly. I'm glad you added the author's note. It clarifies and confirms the determination of this latent spell: earth, sky, water, fire and the crimson passion offered up in supplication to any with eyes to see, ears to hear, mind to think and heart to feel.

What an excellent springboard it makes to jump into that limitless ocean that is you.

Wine and Cheese in the Gallery of Despair

Of course you know that this is an incredibly desperate tone, don't you? The problem for a reader is to discern if art and reality have become blended into this canvas of words in such a way that they might act upon this plea for a Dudley Doright to come to the aid of L'll Nell that has been tied to the railroad tracks by the evil Snidely Whiplash. Do I call the mounties out and try to save poor Nell or do I think of wine & cheese in the gallery of despair and admire the canvas that keeps me guessing about the light that was used to render the reader dazed and confused as to the reality of the drama depicted in this scene? So, on a scale of one to ten - ten being absolute fantasy - where is this piece?

More is Never Enough

I keep reading and then reading again... and again. It's like a new form of heroin that is assimilated, not by the prickly spoonful but by the modulation of photons that impale the eyes with mental glyphs of lingual resonance. Each stanza is a different dime bag of worldly origin; a thing to be unwrapped slowly, carefully; as with a word junky's ritual homage. The product is sniffed, tasted on the tip of the tongue, and then gently warmed to an effervescent bubbling state... until it is ready for that laser-like transit across time and space where it rushes to spread throughout the mind in an intoxicating reverie of electric-like euphoria; then comes the bliss of mysterious, complicated possibilities.

How fitting... my Khan, your visage of poppy field origin that befriends and soothes while chaining the reader to you with this most ancient addiction of the soul. Should we continue to meet in the dark corners of the cafe? The ones where pleasantries are exchanged above the table while small packages slide beneath it from hand to hand... or should I just rat you out to the literati? You know the problem with junkies, don't you? They just keep wanting more and more... and more is never enough.

Effective Success

This, is an imagination breeder. You can't imagine what it bred in my mind. If one of the goals of poetry is to affect the reader then this piece has succeeded; perhaps in ways that were not intended. I'll just leave it at that... it's a poetic success.

Dead Alive

XY, why do you take my ignorant bliss? What did you do with it? Did you store it safely away, to be experienced another day? Did you give it to someone else? Did you use it for yourself? You have placed a heavy stone upon me. I cannot move. I cannot breathe. I am not dead but I am not alive. What is this place? Are you here too? What is next? Is there a next?

Random Context

The denizens of the random context delight in falling upon their zen-blessed swords.

Well-placed Sequins

...and that's the trouble with love versus lust. The marvelous trappings of this piece swing from the high wires without a net. A reader, sitting safely upon the ground, is easily confused by sense of elevation as the thoughts reflect from the well-placed sequins.

Say Play

It brings one up without letting one down. That's the recommended way to start the day; have your say and then go play. Do what you were meant to do with faith and gusto, knowing that you're going to find that equilibrium that is essential for the adventure ahead. Well done, XY.

Memorable Debate

I for one will be impressed when human ideas are debated by minds other than humans. Then they might have a chance of being remembered.

Relatively Absolute

Peace is a human abstraction. Nature confirms this. At best there can only be a momentary equilibrium of forces.

Perhaps you could tell me if you think entropy is absolute or relative?

Chapter 30

Bound Writhing

There are many struggles in life. This is certainly one of them.

Sanctuary

Sad.. the choices people make, the consequences and the places where the mind seeks sanctuary.

Random Me

It feels so much better now.. to know that I am a unique random number in the universe of all random numbers. But am I real or imaginary?

Equal Equality

This is idealism. In actuality, individual equality is an illusion of idealism. An individual within a society is very much like an element within an algebraic equation; metaphorically speaking. It is the mix of operators, variables, values and constants on both sides of an equation that, when solving for a particular variable (person) make it (them) equal. Just as a society both defines and instantiates the concept of 'equality' for an individual within that society.

Destroyer of Souls

Owww... {hugs} ... that pulled something, hard... kind of hurt too. {checking} yes, hurt a lot. I've heard it said that the choices we make in life are things we agreed to do before we were born. Because we had something to learn. I don't know if it's true or not. It's just another one of those things that seems to offer a bit of temporary solace and a shelter from the embarrassment at having made such poor decisions. Fear and doubt; the mind killers and guilt the destroyer of souls.

Necessary Ramparts

Oh, you have a way with the words, don't you? A sterling poem that is crafted as well as any I have seen in this place. The message sounds an ominous tone though and perhaps deserves a thoughtful shudder or a shrug of dread for who may read and not find their thoughts lingering over the necessary ramparts constructed from a lexicon of timeless conflict? I see the picture you've crafted; hanging in this mindful gallery, displayed in thoughtful subdued light. A growing queue awaits the grand opening.

Knowledge Volcano

Aye, and this might be my take on the matter as well for it seems that measurement is the arbiter of reason for a human mind that is at once both a prism and prison for the perception of such things.. such concepts as may rightfully befuddle and confound the new-born. We wail for nourishment from the cosmic teat but hunger still do we all. The volcano of knowledge erupts periodically but the ash of life occludes a satisfying and nourishing comprehension. Well penned, if I may be so bold... friend.

Viable Solutions

Oh my, you do know how to guide that sharp blade, slowly, deftly inward; into the collective consciousness, don't you? I am, almost, embarrassed to reflect what you already know but there are certain demands put upon a reader; such as acknowledgment of perception that resonates within the non-linear portion of the mind. So, this irony and injustice goes on and I, personally, struggle with my own inability to effect any change that might be considered good and worthy by such posterity as may still exist in that future time of reckoning. You have made your point quite clear. I ask, in all humility, have you found anything that is a viable solution set.. especially for M or Q?

(Please, pardon the tone of despair in that last line.)

Nail and Thumb

Yes, I believe it. You spoke to one of them at some point; a dolphin that is. Or, perhaps, using some keenly sharpened empathic ability extracted/reflected the sentiment with the highest probability of righteous resonance fit for human consumption in this time of obvious self-destruction. Although, I cringe at the final line.. the word that draws my thoughts out into the open - "dominant". It seems an oversimplification, a pablum for the young. But the complexity of the thoughts demand simplification and so I have missed the nail and found my thumb. Alas.

Small Recompense

Ha!! Well, this is.. marvelous and an absolutely inspired take on both wisdom and sages as I see it. This is the kind of stuff that I would actually "pay" to read. Go figure, eh? Although, don't get your hopes up.. I think few could buy a loaf with their proceeds in this day and age. Still, there is the occasional genuine admiration from your readership and I certainly count myself among them hence forth. Perhaps that will be some small recompense? ☺

Chapter 31

Befuddle and Discourage

Alas! It seems that if even the most skilled among us are without success in such endeavors can there be any real hope for the rest? An world overflowing with population yet bereft of a comprehensible definition of the abstraction "love" may indicate that failure should not always be viewed as a discouragement. The remainder of your posts here remain, as yet unread, for my perusal but.. I think, X, if I may infer from this piece, that your profile snippet is imbued with a certain amount of needless modesty. To me this is an excellent rendition of the perils of courtship that offers a curious if not insightful glimpse into the dichotomy of conflicting expectations that can befuddle and discourage even the most astute. Thank you for posting! Well done.

Sipping Rent

To abstract and abstraction seems a bit redundant but
you have aged it well within these hallowed casks of myth
and tradition. When sipped slowly it warms and sets the
mind for further contemplations. Perhaps there is a subtle
humor here... but, should I have missed it, I do not care
for here upon my mind is rent these words of thou and
thine and it.

Saucer People

I smile, not with any sort of glee you must understand
but with a smile of understanding. Sad that I did get
it, mostly, the first time around. For the acknowledgment
means a shared context that is very much like lifting the
kimono on the first date.. too brash and forward a thing
to contemplate, especially before the meal is over.

The notes are appreciated though as they add both clarity and confirmation to the great mystery of it all upon first
reading. Also, they encourage one to pass through it again
matching up the elements as the intent solidifies within the
mind. Rather strange. Rather nice.

How was San Diego this time of year? Have the saucer
people come to steal your brain yet? ☺

River Blossom

A curious piece. It smacks of a compulsion to visit the
closet confessional and relate some pesky semblance of
guilt for a private conversation that was being thought

but could not be spoken. On the other hand, perhaps it is more the response to a series of lets-get-to-know-each-other questions; like those that are thrust upon the new tenants of classroom seats each season. A firm new blossom, falling into the river of life... your destiny awaits you.

Brutal Days

How does one go about reviewing something like this? As I have written in reviews before, perhaps once or twice, I always find it interesting what an author chooses to post as their first work; to share with the world, so to speak. Often I find that these pieces define the mind, the character and the essence of who that person is and if not who they are now then who they may become. If there is conflict it is with all who may happen upon this piece and read it from their own personal perspective and world experiences. There may be a momentary resolution of personal emotion for both the writer and the reader but the story itself is as old as man; as old as war. Yet this reads as young and fresh and brutal and real as the bravest and best that are (still) sent to, "..carry out the deeds their words desired." And as for those, rest assured, the days are "..coming for you.."

Fling, Flang, Flung

Do you want affirmation and encouragement or do you want a real review; like your teacher might give you? I say this only because you have "flung" (and I use that word kindly) up a few lines of dialog and while they are rather nice, for the most part, they beg the question, "What are you trying to do with them?" What is your goal? Having read your comments to the other reviewers it seems that you will not be getting back to this start up sketch anytime soon because you are burdened with an overabundance of homework. Alas.

So, I'll leave you with these thoughts. It is reasonably well written. It has mistakes. It's too short to really care much about the characters. There is no background. It seems to fit your sphere of reality (from what I can tell). I'm sure we could be friends. You'll find I always try to tell the truth in the very best way possible. I do not always succeed. ☺

Exploring Rum

Oh curious mysteries.. so comfortable where they sleep in dark, earthy unknown. Your poetry will be the seed for much bounty; so it seems to appear through the rum glass half full. A Caravaggio in miniature this.. I shall pin it here, just to the side of my explorers compass.

Small Sharps

I'm delighted when I stumble upon an opening in the mind where the being manifest therein smiles out upon the darkness and forces it to withdraw in a ponderous, thoughtful cringe. It is a strategy that has proven its worth time and time again in that eternal back-and-forth between day and night, wrong and right, friend and foe.. things hidden and things revealed. The knife is small but the blade is sharp.

Island Flowers

From innocence blooms desire.. the world's afire about this azure ringed domain but within these timeless gardens and pools where the sun sparkles bright.. three souls intertwine and bind the essence of being.. together as one.. becoming more. With smiles that ravage the eyes, murmured sighs entertain the imagination of this unbound trepiece. A tender touch of freedom that caresses the heart of both young and old. Treasure each other and so it will be.. forever. An amazing thing to share oh lovely island flowers!

Blushing Tomatoes

X! You sly tease.. making the tomatoes blush. Nice one. ☺

Read and Bleed

I would love to read some author's notes on this piece. Very vivid and intense but hopelessly whipped by the imagery, to and fro, in this storm of bloody metaphor. The only straws for this reader to clutch to have been driven through the tree that stands in this forest of life and death. Is it so painful that we must bandage our own wounds suffered in trying to understand this piece. Perhaps there is less to understand than I imagine. Perhaps it's simply about color; the color of blood and things that blend in similar hues as a world horizon screams of sunset just there, where life ends. Who knows? Certainly not this reader. All I can do is read and bleed in sympathy; for what it's worth.

Chapter 32

Elmo Brainfluff

Not unsuitable for readers under 18. This is Tickle-me-Elmo brainfluff. Something created, as you say, when cleaning out the old hard drive one day when there was nothing better to do. The sad part is that it has no message, no story, no rhyme, no reason (that I can see) other than to fill up white space. But, I could just be missing the big picture. Which is it?

Transcendental Metronome

Why do all the good ones go unread.. for so long too? It's a mystery. Oh well, I'm happy to say that someone (this one) discovered you here and became engrossed in your Transcendental Metronome. For the life of me I cannot see what is here that would ever merit a +18 or over rating unless you were concerned about the one word that's used so much it's even part of the liturgy. An excellent poem,

X. I wonder if you're still around?

You're Welcome

You're welcome. Just remember, blood is neither Democrat or Republican, Black or White, Left or Right... it's that spot on the ground, where you stand; the punch-out from the ticket that bought your admission to this American Theater.

Logical Linkage

Well, I'm glad you were able to at least have it make sense, mostly. So much stuff that is thrown up here is psycho-mind-babble; I know, I've done it.. I do it. But I hope that occasionally someone will give it the benefit of the doubt as I do here. It takes some effort, some twice-thrice reading but eventually something will fall out that we can latch on to. Here there are lots of ropes dangling from the rafters. Fortunately the bats are having no trouble sleeping; metaphorically speaking. I have no criticism for you at this time. I think, however, that you are the type that will always be your own worst critic. Therein lies the danger, no? Too much.. to little, where is the balance? Clearly the message needs some logical linkage lest we hang ourselves from the things that clutter this dark room. If we're peeking into the mind of the sleep deprived then so be it. If this is just paid passage through the fun house then a little day-glow tape on the floor, to lead the way, would be helpful.

Pleasing Articulations

This poem was curiously coy and somewhat brusque in the beginning, emotionally speaking; but the second stanza won me over completely.

It voices a candid honesty that cuts to the chase; as in when there is a value placed upon time and upon knowing what's important to this particular type of relationship. The title really says it all doesn't it? The sonnets, love songs, and operas all have their day in the sun but if you wish to be both endearing and enduring then demonstrate an observant and discerning nature; an appreciation for both mind and body. In particular, understand that there is a premium placed upon sharing values that acknowledge a sense of the human place in the cosmos, an admiration and understanding for the nature of an existence that incorporates the essential elements of love and learning that, by nature, must evolve or perish. In all probability these things will occur for what were the chances that you would write and we should read?

Perhaps there is some truth to the thought that nothing is ever really "finished"... that it just seemed the best place to stop at the time.

A pleasing articulation, XX.

Time Tubes

Well, this one certainly evokes a plethora of emotion! As I contemplate and re-read my mind does a logical juxtaposition of telescoping time tube examinations and postulations from each end of history. An excellent example in the spirit of Tovli as I understand it. Thank you, XX!

Hidden Forces

I like it as a sketch of a scene in a story that is waiting to be born. Perhaps you should consider where you want to take this. What are you trying to achieve in this scene? Introduce characters? Describe a set of feelings/emotions? Setup a part of a plot? The words are fine. The simile and metaphor are adequate. It needs "purpose." Why is the character where they are, doing what they're doing? Why is the protagonist doing what their doing? Is it revenge? Are they deranged or psychopathic? Where are we? Is it daylight or dark? Does that matter? What does matter? These are the things that you must think about if you want to improve as a writer. Writer's write because they have something they want to communicate. Sometimes what they want to communicate isn't in the stories or the poems that they write; not directly at least. Often these reasons, in the end, make the most compelling stories. Consider your reasons for writing. Why do you write? It's for a friend. I know. You said that. But, what are the expectations? For you, for your friend? Where and what is the conflict? What overt or hidden forces have compelled you to write this piece? I know... too many questions. But they're intended as friendly questions. This.. this is me

smiling.. friend?

Hypnotic Grandeur

"Love poems aren't my forte..." - but you did this one so well, XX!! The muse likes you today. You had me hypnotized with those words.. I was seeing things that weren't there.. like I was the volunteer from the audience in a hypnotist's routine. Only there wasn't anything routine about this poem. You, seriously I say, have expressed some of the ethereal insight that is necessary to experience the grandeur of it all. But that's just my take on it.. tonight. ☺

Psychotropic Beetles

My dear XX,

I don't know which one I will insult more by this. You or XY. At first I thought that perhaps XX-2 was ghostwriting under an alias (yes, she's that good – and crazy) but then I thought, "OK, let's go with the flow." By the time I was midway through I was on a parallel track, pondering the possibilities inspired by the story ... would XY wish to go to South America? Is she liken unto a super model? (Duh.. probably, sure.) Would see be the one to listen attentively to a campfire lecture on curious cultural passion rituals? Um, sure. Why not (stylistic splendor)? Of course I had just come fresh from reading your script about the Iowa hog farm and this seemed somewhat a non-sequitur – but forging onward through this jungle of words I came finally to that little white building and stopped for a sip in the lounge while our hero braided a twisted ending that roped my visual cortex back into the jungle. I think it was my curious reader skills that transposed my identity of self with the main character, if only for a moment. The feel of beetles crawling up my nostrils was almost more than I could endure. With a strength-of-will equaled only by he who lay prone upon the common ground of an obscure jungle village I assimilated that hallucinogenic ending and began reliving the euphoria of the piece in toto. As I write this I now find myself with the strange desire to fish out some calipers and measure the gap between my sanity and the reality that I have just been subjected to. Even now I am pondering the sales potential of a well-crafted sitcom ... the title is everything you know. Perhaps, "XY and the X" or just "X XY." What do you think?

Chapter 33

Typewriter Brooms

I love this, XY! I really, really do. It makes me want to invest in Real Estate somewhere. Perhaps New York, a block on 5th Avenue or maybe somewhere in Brooklyn. The whole block devoted to coffee shops, bakeries, bookstores, boutiques for sequin'd pumps and $10,000 fountain pens sold only with magic ink. The kind that flows from the freshly opened wounds of poets and writers of human angst. I wonder if the police would even dare enter there?

Frigid Fantasies

The polar bears and penguins are up early this morning. I see the bears rummaging through the mail bags, looking for those specials packages of treats that go well with the morning coffee. The penguins are still hunkered down, keeping their feet warm and dreaming of the sea... (does the sea see me or do I see the sea?) There is life and death upon the sheets. One's cold death, another's warm life. On the bright, flickering, dancing side you've made even the news cheerful and that's rather difficult to do these days. I wonder what the emperor thinks about -170F temperatures and gale-force winds? Fantasies of ice bowling balls and penguin pens... sooo glad it's toasty inside this hovel (at the moment). ☻

Mixed Menus

What an odd use of a medium name. I'm trying to contrast it with "oil" love or "water color/colour" love or ... whatever. The only thing I can come up with is the time it takes to fix the love onto the canvas in a permanent state. Acrylic is much faster than oils - perhaps less so than water color/colour. So is this it then? The love was "quick" to set? Or perhaps the love was quick to dry, set and fly (away)? It's a mystery. Oh you poets with layer upon layer of hidden metaphor. What ever shall we do with you? MENU: Fresh boiled poet in metaphor sauce.

Cherry Mysts

This seems a deadly mix for a gaze into the morning mist. I lift the cup to my lips and then sip... in a moment there is this sense of "toxic intoxication and blush'd smoke" that seems to leave the mind riven. I lift my cup again to this...

Peaceful Smiles

Such is the struggle of life in whatever form we choose to see it. Animal, vegetable or mineral. Humans are animals too, aren't they? Beware the weeds of dawn e're thoughts upon them fawn.

Mirrored Views

I see in this a fanciful seriousness that yearns to share insight into the nature of woman. The articulations and word choice render the subject modern and archaic simultaneously; probably an intentional dichotomy. For man, to understand woman (or woman to understand herself for that matter) is the quintessential expression of man's eternal ignorance. It is as the blind striving to see the divine and yet there are those occasional threads of light that appear in the dark behind closed eyes... and these may originate as much from the true soul of humanity as in the random chemistry of body and brain. The interpretation is as challenging as watching a kitten unravel a ball of yarn and with humorous, smiling desperation try to make some sense of its pattern of play and design of string upon the floor. A Monet? A Van Gogh? No, to this timid reader it seems more of lines in sympathy with the work of Dame Barbara Hepworth and perhaps that is where this should end for to add more would certainly take away its honorable intent. I exit the gallery of your lines as silent as a church mouse stealing away from the kitchen, knowing that I am soon to partake in a feast of reflection.

To X's question, perhaps it is a keyboard code page

translation problem. Most likely, Ms. XY may elucidate, the intent is to use an interpunct[1]. Now, back to the poem.

— In reply:

You really do leave the kindest and wonderfully detailed reviews, many thank yous. I originally wrote this as prose, then it became an overlong whatever, is now condensed into yes, a touch of the modern and archaic because, as we all know She has been around for more than a while and yet has evolved into the same but different woman.. you noticed that, and ten out of ten for doing so. One day I might write or try to write a similar piece on Man [34].. but how to finish!!! Happy Monday.

Pretty Plumes

In the movie, Under The Tuscan Sun, there is a scene where this (being struck by bird splat) occurs. According to the locals, this brings good fortune to the unfortunate. This might explain a lot. Why people are superstitious... why I haven't been to the beach lately... why they say, "Unlucky at cards - unlucky at love." Why do large hands

---

1. An interpunct, also called an interpoint, is a punctuation mark consisting of a dot used for interword separation in ancient Latin script and in some modern languages as a stand-alone sign inside a word. http://en.wikipedia.org/wiki/Interpunct

require large pockets? Though I had a large rubber band
my plane would not fly for it was propless.

Glory Fonts

It climbs the mountain but takes the tortuous route I'm
afraid. There are crags within the nooks and crannies... a
fractal landscape that is nearly barren but here and there
a sprig of moss or lichen and the occasional pile of stones
from pilgrims that passed the same way many times before
but long ago – their bones, bleached and white upon the
same slopes – all hoping to attain that illusive summit.

Maroon Tiltings

Two phrases stood out for me because of their mystery:

- "The heart has its reasons of which reason knows
  nothing"

- protect'd enlighten'd shadows

I see the quote has caught other's attention too so I vote
for provocation as well. But what does it provoke in me? I
see spiders in space trying to spin their webs but gravity
is lacking, The fly is in heaven as it has but to flap it's
wings to gain traction while the spider must cling to its
thread and hope for the satisfaction of attraction. Static
on all channels as the sound of hearts-a-flutter breech the
dark, winsome night.

Dainty Bands

Rings... such a symbolic form and used for so many in-
numerable and varied reasons. This poem reaches for that
dusty archetype and seeks to do justice by it. It's simplicity
is it's strength - that and the imagery and form bound with
the purposeful message. Nicely done, X.

Chapter 34

Velvet Chirps

You may have said this to or perhaps thought this about someone, "I liked it better when you were crazy." But if not, well then, never mind. It segues nicely with your author's note don't you think?

Dorka Floobins

It's amazing, isn't it? The inebriation of altered perspective. I adore your vocabulary. Phonic-based transliterations... the mind, so mailable, so adaptive. The ability to overlay learned patterns of thought upon an alien existence and actually have it make a sort of sense. You do good work, XX. I will recommend you for entrance into The Pharsthunk Academy. I look forward to attending your graduation ceremonies near the pylon of Nute in about four Sols. Until then, be well and puque lots.

Blue Barks

It has a nice rhythm, easy to dance to. It screams silently with multiple levels of alliteration, simile, metaphor, carnivores cavorting about, "...in the middle of the night." What a fright; the sight of light.

Invisible Creature-features

I would like to say, "I took it all in stride." Yea. Right. But it did compel me to share something with you that you may not be aware of and although the question has been asked many times before, by almost everyone, even those that it has affected directly, it is this... Do yo know WHY, "Angelic travelers (who) carry probes in their back-packs?" Because in a bad automobile accident, when they must use the jaws of life bystanders see that it's not the container that's important but rather what's INSIDE that counts. So in like fashion when Angelic Travelers use those back-pack probes on unsuspecting humans it's like that. It's the tiny little organisms in your INSIDES that are important. They're just trying to preserve and maintain the oldest, most intelligent living creatures on this planet... bacteria. Humans are just engineered vehicles that convey colonies about in a self-repairing environment. The human body is just a ship for their thriving micropolii. That's why there is no thought given to pain when the probes come out. Do you even consider the pain of the automobile as the jaws-of-life rip through it's construction in order to free the ugly-bags-of-mostly-water that are trapped, inside, bleeding, crying out in pain and agony, "God, help us!" Blood flowing - that's the RED ALERT of the mitochlorian force-wielders - the equivalent of Armageddon at the molecular and subatomic level. Have a heart XX. It's just a big pump anyway you look at it.

Tolken Kittens

I will remember these vivid words. They remind me of the distant past when the Bong show was still flitting it's pre-idol excellence outward through the solar system, beyond Saturn and into the cosmic great beyond.

Absolute Truths

So, what you have taught me is that we are not alone in this conflict of the heart. Perhaps more than this is the thought it instils - that one of best qualities of humanity is the ability to see ourselves in others and commiserate with a compassion that is (perhaps) uniquely human. Yes, we may laugh but that is often only a response to a (nearly) incomprehensible situation - in many cases - but I'm sure there are as many opportunities for joy and laughter (the good kind) as there are for love.

I love it when you (seem to) talk "teacherie." It makes me want to "exchange", to commiserate, to read more of your thoughts and to have "interesting conversation" - even if only as writer/reader. You are treasure beyond words.

Urges Struggling

I think perhaps the shadow people have invaded your cobweb spaces. Consider the flower, how it wilts and the cow how it moos and why. Imagine the truth of lies become reality and ask yourself if it was all worth it?

Honest Feelings

It may be that in years to come an understanding will flood upon you. These things you write of are both common and unique to this time, this place and to you. You may understand that it takes time and things, moments that are not these - that perhaps are the antithesis of these to really appreciate them. This piece seems a clear and honest statement of "now." ...and that's OK. We do not love the world and expect anything in return. We love the world and all it is, both light and dark, because we can... because it is in us to do so.

Purple Streams

Erotica seems to mold itself to the unique characteristics of the writer. I think this is no exception. I find it brash, experimental and gentle with only a touch of unnecessary roughness. The panoply of sense-keys do not go unnoticed. They are not mere adornment or useless, flailing appendages. No, they have purpose and a life of their own. So reach out again, with your pen and touch someone.

Buzzing Thoughts

> *I'd build you up and make you whole.*
> *I'd recommend you with a*
> *voice that's bold.*
> *If you die, I'd surely cry and take your*
> *ashes out unto the sea where*
> *waves could gently dance with*
> *thee.*
> *I'd hold you dear within my heart and*
> *your memory would be only*
> *the start for in the twilight fly-*
> *ing by light of a blazing corpse*
> *I should be sobbing, crying.*
> *For what heart could ever dance again*
> *with glee after knowing true*
> *love and the beloved bee?*

Altered Lives

I remember, not so long ago, how you were chided from the sidelines for chipping away at that large block of stone in your special garden. It was only half-finished but the form of woman appeared in due time and it caused no small amount of consternation within the mind and hearts of those random travelers passing by.[33] Now you have hewn the other half, this time with broader, heavier tools that require a firm grasp, strength and perseverance to render with fidelity that n-dimensional montage that lay dormant yet growing all these years. It speaks, upon completion, of its own accord and in so doing silences any simpering criticism of pose or posture or other mundane observations of the lesser-learned or lesser experienced.

In consideration may I suggest an appropriately crafted and placed sitting bench? ...just there, near the flowers. I think it may be required; to provide a temporary respite for those that, in passing, feel compelled to stop and then have difficulty moving on. They may desire a well-positioned spot from which to further contemplate its message and adjust the thoughtful shadows that trace its base and their ever-mindful memories.

— In reply:

OH, dear one.. your reviews are works of art, they really are! Thank you for such musical comments.. all I can reply is that I've tried to stand in other's shoes.. considerably larger than mine too. Having brothers and long-time friends helped.. but doubt that i've really touched those feelings so many feel at some time in their lives. Humans are complex creatures because they've been forced to be by society and upbringing.. sad.. sad. Thank you for every word.. truly.

Melding Strums

The search for a soul-mate, whatever their qualities may be in our minds, imagined, cannot come to fruition without a certain modicum of self-doubt. However, there is an unfathomable need to place undue trust in the universe-at-large for it is this that often appears as an insurmountable obstacle to beings that, for brief moments of their on-again/off-again existence, careen through the mind of words; their goal to purge and reconstitute "things" ... or worse, feelings and thoughts that have scurried away to the dark corners. They hide there, trembling like tiny mice stalked by the fur and fangs of monumental torment and grief turned unbearable anguish. Still, you have scry'd some that beg consideration. The psalm, the balm, the night, the light ... and the living beings, the him and her that think occasionally of each other. If only they could find a common branch upon which to rest those storm-battered wings. Perhaps then a new paradigm might be discovered while conceding things past and perhaps, things yet to come. In lyric mind one may hope, seek and sometimes find. Eh, XX?

Part III

Review Exercises

Chapter 35

Practice Material

The following pieces, mainly poems and a few short stories, are included as fodder for those readers that wish to practice reviewing ideas they may have obtained by examination of the exemplar reviews in the previous section. They are varied in theme and style but should be easily critiqued. While they are in no way meant to stand on their own merits, some may actually succeed in that respect; for that we can offer no reasonable explanation. Additional insight may be gleaned by sharing reviews of the practice material and comparing notes with others that may be so inclined.

Chapter 36

Poems - I

Changes

CHANGES

In... the window a pane is broken

> *creeps the cold air and dust*
> *crawls a small insect token*
> *pours the rain and rusts*

The.. iron mask upon a face

> *change a sudden start*
> *slender chain entangled waist*
> *iron clasps upon a heart*

Fall... broken to the floor

through a breathless wind
singing who adores
and lives to love again

Sailing San Diego

SAILING SAN DIEGO

Sailing thru and round the waves
Not too high, not too cold
Pretty sailors ply their trade
Not to shy, not too bold.

Golden streamers intertwine
About the sun, just for fun
Finger clouds above the brine
Caress the days, every one.

Polished Pieces

POLISHED PIECES

I polished it to pieces
This little verse of mine.
I polished it to pieces
Just so that it would rhyme.

It broke as I polished it
And rubbed so very hard
But even thought it's broken
It's hard to discard.

I cherished those little pieces
Each and every one
For I gathered them all up
On the end of my thumb

And I put them back within
The tip of my quill pen
And I took a brief respite
Before I wrote again.

Magnetic Poetry

MAGNETIC POETRY

You   manipulate   lick
          love to elaborate   when we
          lust and be
I   incubate   dream
Delirious luscious together pink and
          think

of delicate essential death

The Destiny of St. Goodbye

THE DESTINY OF ST. GOODBYE

You're such a difficult thing!
Difficult not to love
Difficult to let go of.

Go and spread your wings
Jump off the bough
Into the now

Run, swim and sing

Be the eagle in the sky
A voice that never lies

Then as life may bring
So do what you must
Being kind, merciful and just.

Graduation Day

GRADUATION DAY

In stars and stripes you walked today

With outstretched hand on grassy ways

Toward a future full of promise.

The Voice Inside

THE VOICE INSIDE

A-MUSE-MENT : Thoughts, inspirations (of the "Muses" and such) taken to heart and given to mankind that they might profit by them (it's a lame definition but it will do for now).

I: The voice is the master.

THE VOICE: No. Not necessarily, says I. I prefer to think of myself as one who points out the possibilities. Your free will is master here. Gaze into the crystal. Tell me what you see.

I: I see the realms of Fire, Earth, Water, and Air.

THE VOICE: Explain.

I: The red of the sunrise and sunset, signifying the fire deep within the bowels of the Earth. For every sunrise there is a sunset. As each opportunity is lost so a new one presents itself. As something lives, so must it die. Each player shall have their turn.

THE VOICE: What is the way?

I: It is the way of Thyngz.

THE VOICE: Good! Now tell me, tell yourself, when do you hear my voice?

I: Only when myne own is silent. When my mind is calm and clear as crystal.

THE VOICE: Excellent! Continue. Describe the realm.

I: The Green is the living Earth and all that dwell upon and in the land, which is dark as death and Black. Life and death are one and the same experience.

THE VOICE: Pray, continue. and the Blue?

I: The Blue is the Ocean of Truth that surrounds and envelopes the land, without which all life should perish. The death of fire is rock which is consumed by the sea that it might become a bed for life.

THE VOICE: .and the Air?

I: The Air is the crystal, the crystal is the Air. Conduit of energy, highway of the elements.

THE VOICE: .and the towers? Do you see the towers?

I: Yes. They are the edifice of mankind that stand upon the land and sink beneath the sea.

THE VOICE: And the flea. what of the flea?

I: The flea is here to make a mockery of me and my imperfect existence. For every one I kill, ten more spring up to take its place. They represent the seemingly infinite fortitude of life.

THE VOICE: What is the way?

I: It is the way of Thyngz. Are there any others?

THE VOICE: As I mentioned. you know, you really are

doing quite well. I didn't expect you to remember half this much. As I was saying, there are the ways of Truth, Justice, Beauty, Love and so on and for each of these there is an alternate path. Light and Dark. Dark and Light.

I: Who's to say which is which? Isn't it merely a matter of definition?

THE VOICE: Do you remember when you gazed into each chamber of the crystal? Do you recall the second chamber and what you described therein?

I: Yes. It was the face of Truth and Logic. A tormented visage. A face with one good eye that reflected alternately red and blue. The red representing the lust for knowledge and blue, the truth to know it when found. The other eye (I) was sealed shut. Blinded by Logic and the mouth, open wide, howling in despair (at its plight).

THE VOICE: All in all, a good nights work. Now, go to sleep. Perhaps we shall talk again.

I: .indeed.

On Education

ON EDUCATION

The crystal dog and gossamer cat
Sat near the window sill
And the child that came
To school that day
Declared they'd had their fill

Of reading, writing, and arithmetic
And subjects so arcane
That should they be lost In a great abyss
That heart would feel no pain.

To see them lost forever
Beneath a soggy, oozing mass
Overgrown with briar and bramble,
Tall trees and waving grass.

Forniclaise

FORNICLAISE

Beneath the iron of churlish flask
The helbrin's darg he took to task.
With brazen and unbridled cold
T'was told to all, both young and old.

Forearm thrust wildly to the sky
And neck thrown back as if to cry
But halting only dids't he this;
The lonely whimper of thin lips.

As liquid pass'd with steamy kiss
To gather speed on journeyed gliss,
Splattering, dribbled off the tong
And fell upon the table long.

From blazing log to embered sea
At last cried he, "Brehaa I be!"
And cast his eye about the room
Towards the fire and thundrust broom.

His thoughts, stirred only from within,
By mounds of gold that might have been
And numbing now the memory
He sits with gaze turned glassily.

Upon the table warpped and bent
Reek'd with hell's own foul ferment
Lies branded deep within the glaze
The empty oath of Forniclaise.

Remorse

REMORSE

Come fill the space within my heart
That in the darkness dwells.
With light and love rescue this dove
From the burning pit of hell.

A pit that burns with dark remorse
In flame that gives no light
Above the ash of what might have been
That was just and good and right.

Empty Wells

EMPTY WELLS

The well is empty. Toll the bell.
Turn the handle slowly

As though the bucket were full.
Listen to the windlass creak
While the rope embraces the dusty
                rounds.

Lift the bucket from the dark hole
And set it on the stone surround.
Dip your fingers deep within
And pull them slowly out
Yielding not to the impatience of youth.

On Sunday Drives

ON SUNDAY DRIVES

It's cold in the back seat of the car
The grays, blues, and browns of a
Snowless countryside in
Winter pass by the wrap-around
Screen of the rear window glass.

There's a lot of room between
My knees and the front seat
Where you sit beside him.
Talking, chattering, saying nothing
In particular as you glance
Occasionally from his face

To the black road ahead.

I raise my hand to touch the
Velvet surface of the roof-liner
And, predictably, I am admonished
As my finger traces across
His field of vision in the rear-view
Mirror.

Lots of ashtrays... I wonder how many
    cigarettes they have to smoke
    to fill them all up?

Reading

READING

Slowly! Read me, slowly! Let the
Words form the sound in your mind.
Do not hasten through them as a
Dog gulping down its food.
Yes, you are a quick study but
I am old
And have learned the value of
Savoring the moment. A lesson
Wasted on many of not nearly
My years.

Take a deep breath and glance
Away from these words.
Return and visit them once again,
Stroked like the cat in your lap
Until they purr with contentment.
If you are too warm, enjoy the coolness
Of the night and the full moon rising
Behind the shadow of the redwoods
on the dry hillside.

Lift your hands toward the stars and
                    feel
The mists of dark skys pass
Through your fingers and over your
                    hands.
Reach out with finger and thumb
As if to grasp the planets;
The space within, a measure of your
                    life.

The Moon Is Full

THE MOON IS FULL

The moon is full But you are empty.
Cold and distant Are the eyes that
Once gazed with Warmth and approval

At this now sullen face.

Dizzy rats fall up stairs
Where you comb your hair
Near underwear, long
Overdue at the laundry.

Weathered cement, cold
And gray, crumbling,
Littered with the small
Purple bodies of berries
From trees unconcerned
With the reckless heels
Of hard leather boots.

Kiss the rim of brown bottles.
Caress the channel changer
Remote stations warn of storm
But they cannot save you.

Winter Sleep

WINTER SLEEP

Smooth and bare
Breast of goddess
A vision it is true
And as I sit

Mean Not to stare
Yet picture only you.

Red rose of spring
Hot summer spray
Georgeious forest fall
A diamond in my winter sleep
A moment to recall.

Lost Cargo

LOST CARGO

Who speaks with such quick tongue
That the lark seems a plodding beast of
          burden?
What can be said will be said, If not by
          you
Then who? Pray tell.

To close mine eyes
And hear your voice
Close within my mind
That is my punishment.

There is a place within
Where your tongue lies
Wagging, yapping, like

The shrill bark of a small dog.

And I seek to employ
Every contrivance of imagination
To fabricate a suitable and effective
       muzzle
But with no success.

How often must good fortune
Have sailed steadfastly toward thy open
       port
Only to be confused and
Diverted at the last moment

Thinking it would surely run aground,
Beached near an applauding troupe of
Mean-tempered spectators
Bent upon reselling lost cargo.

The Reading Room

THE READING ROOM

There is a room, both warm and soft
With sturdy beams, ceiling cross'd
Where sun hangs fixed, t'ween earth
       and cloud

In frozen time, near window's shroud

Where quill and ink, book and paper
Commune together in silent measure
And thoughts linger, if but a moment
Paying tribute to forgotten poets

Authors of strange and ragged verse
Bound dry in tomes of lyric terse
The world for this may be the worse

At knowing not in greater depth and
Caring less that upon each and every
                    breast
Have fallen tears of sorrow
And, perhaps, some of happiness

They linger still among the shelves
Rediscovered by singular folk
That through volumes dig and delve
Until, for some by fortunes stroke

They chance upon a single note
A bell thought that ringing clear
Signs deaf from hearts, another tear

Dark Love Burning

DARK LOVE BURNING

We sing the strings of darkness
Planets fleeing their moons
Yet captured by the sun
In unrelenting eccentricities.

I flee from you my moon goddess
But there is no escape.
The rape of your madness draws me.
Near violent moments repeating
Throughout eternity for all to see

And as quickly as any instant can be
Thrust away, doomed to repeat
This sad, sad charade.

Far off in space, you race and
Reach your aphelion.
Pausing in time that never exists
You gaze at the wonders
Of the universe sublime.

You remember our dark love
Burning, smoldering
On the altar of the unforgiven and
Once again, start slowly the race

Toward another place where
With the heat of your body near
We rekindle our passion.

Sweet form and mass of delicate de-
      struction
Come near within my grasp and
Lay quietly, here, above me.
Let me exert the strength
Of unseen fingers and hands
Over the dark side of your surface
While I ply the kiss
You've never before experienced
Upon the roundness of your sunlit
      shoulder.

Turn your face toward me, once again
And feel this dark love, burning
Press your lips to mine anew, in inno-
      cence
And think no thoughts, but only feel
Lest the spell that is the moment
Be broken and once thus broken
I am forced by nature to endure
The pain that is knowing
Your absence

The Visit

The Visit

Come, visit me in the country
Leave the city where it belongs
Lost in the din of breathless insanity
Find your way out of the throng

If it is dark when you arrive
Step softly and lift the latch
Find your comfort near the hearth
Beneath this roof of thatch

Tomorrow, when you awake
Your company I shall keep
And the heavy burdens that you carry
Will be lighter before you sleep

With pleasant conversation
And cheerful mirth and song
We shall guide each others spirits
Until shadows cast are long

A River Lies Between Us

A RIVER LIES BETWEEN US

A river lies between us
Silent, swift and deep
Upon one side the sun arises
And upon the other, sleeps

Upon one side the sun arises
With promises great and bold
And upon the other, as it sets
Naught but gray and cold

A river few dare to cross
Or venture there within
For danger lies at every turn
Promising only uncertain ends

To any poor soul of mortal clay
That near these banks should stray
And lose their footing, fall therein
Only to be swept away

By mighty passion'd currents
So terrible and strong
That few, if any, can escape
And then so not for long

To clutch at passing moments
And even to forsake
To win again the other shore
And life anew retake

A river lies between us
Silent, swift and deep
It beckons with a soothing call
Through emptiness and grief

With promises of comfort
To all who would embrace
A slender song voiced silently
In waking and in sleep

Of soft and gentle memories
Of times and places past
Of innocence and virtue
A pure and fragile glass

That slips from aging fingers
To break upon the ground
The shattered remnant from thus
Are forged eternal crowns

Love Circles

Love Circles

Cold, rainy, streets, night
Black, shiny, neon lights
Harsh words, lovers fight

Anger walks, splashing fast
Who said what, last
Remorse, regret, slowly pass

Insane, reason without will
Guilty conscience, feel ill
Hatred, shame, heart fill

Soaking, chilled, slowly stalking
Silent shadows, homeward walking
Sullen eyes, silent talking

Anger melts, courage driven
Pouting lips, hand given
Tears, embrace, each forgiven

Chapter 37

Poems - II

Stick Bang Pow

Stick Bang Pow

Lunch at the Cafe Liberty

with apologies to Emma Lazarus.

Planes land, trains arrive, ships dock
...
Everyone gets off eventually. Some
with
a throbbing head full of stories or
just ideas of jumbled words seek-
ing the affinity

Of an auspicious close coupling.

Take a ticket, queue by the picket
Or jump, crawl, slither, sit ... be com-
                    miserate
Along the inconspicuous walls or
On the dance floors where the music of
                    simile and metaphor
Blare   notes   written   with   the   ink   of
                    leaking thoughts.

Or, if you prefer, become a voyeur's
                    watch
Telling the time as character outlines
Swim through fluid plots of conflicting
                    tension.
We find our way here, each in their own
                    way and time
With   hearted   sleeves   plastered   upon
                    load-bearing rhymes.

Silly-seeking a reeking of approval, lu-
                    cent sympathetic eyes
To look upon our plight and proffer a
                    care and
In so doing, service our vehicle of life
That we, some being human, others not
                    so much,
Are forced by nature to share.

The lunch menu at The Cafe Liberty -
rewritten each day.
Having trouble choosing? I recommend
the sample platter of
Stick Bang Pow ... it seems to go well
With The dull matter of existence that,
Over time, becomes, who we truly are;
not who we wish to be.

Pencil Masts

PENCIL MASTS

Beneath a squirrel infested tree
A wordy word-mangler lingers;
The mangler, a cheerful lass she,
With sticky, s'mores-inked fingers;
And page-keeps from basket lair
Are treasured by feathered singers.

Her hair twisted into lovers knots
Her face blooms as rose or daisy;
Her nose is wet with honest snot,
For to wipe she is too lazy,
And writes of vamps, blood and lace
For she knows they are all crazy.

Day in, day out, from dusk till light,

You can hear her nasal bellows;
You can hear her scratch, plot and fight
With sharpened ink-sticks of willow,
Like a mouse with cheese in full flight,
Seeking quickly to its pillow.

And mates roving class-to-class
Look at her large eyes glistening;
They love to hear her flaming crass,
About some character wots missing
And in passing catch muttered words
Like snakes in baskets hissing.

She goes on some days to a bog
And sits among the pale Lilies;
She hears the splash of bird and frog,
She hears the wee folk being silly
Singing as in a hollow log,
And it gives her the willies.

It sounds just like another's snore,
One heard long ago in a cave
She needs must think of him once more,
Now in a distant land he shaves;
And with his Montblanc as an oar
Rows through words as he raves.

Laughing, crying, in their dreams of
                    flying
Through her characters they will live;

Each morning sees some a sighing,
Each evening a write she'll give
Something written - honest trying,
She's earned her right to be so glib.

Thanks, thanks to thee, my scribing
lass,
For with thy mangled words I'm well
tossed
And when my zenith sun is past
Such memories shall not be lost
Your ship of dreams with pencil masts
Shall keep me safe within your
thoughts.

Eight Ball

EIGHT BALL

Q: Will I ever be rich and famous?
A: "Without a doubt."

Woohoo!

Q: Can money buy love?
A: "My reply is no."

You and the Beatles ...

Q: *Is there life after death?*
A: *"Yes."*

Q: *Is there a God?*
A: *"Yes."*

Q: *Is there a devil?"*
A: *"Yes."*

Q: *Does love conquer all?"*
A: *"It is decidedly so."*

Q: *Is anybody going to read this?*
A: *"Yes - definitely."*

Q: *Will they believe it?*
A: *"Ask again later."*

Q: *Is the meaning of life knowable?*
A: *"Most likely."*

Q: *Does life exist elsewhere in the universe? A: "Most likely."*

Q: *Am I the smartest person that ever lived? A: "Most likely."*

Q: *Do you have a sense of humor?*

A: "Ask again later."

Q: Do you always tell the truth?
A: "You may rely on it."

Q: Do you ever lie?
A: "Most likely."

Q: Are you human?
A: "Don't count on it."

Q: Are UFOs real?
A: "Better not tell you now."

Q: Is sleep good?
A: "Without a doubt."

Q: Will there be a tomorrow?
A: "As I see it, yes."

Q: I am thinking of a number between
zero and infinity; what is it."
A: "Concentrate and ask again."

Q: Will I ever know true love?
A: "Yes - definitely."

Q: ...in my lifetime?
A: "You may rely on it."

Q: *Are you sure you always tell the truth?*
A: *"Signs point to yes."*

Q: *Do good and evil exist?*
A: *"Outlook good."*

Q: *Is it better to be good than evil?*
A: *"Yes - definitely."*

Q: *Will I always know if something is good or evil?*
A: *"Cannot predict now."*

Q: *Do you ever get tired of answering questions?*
A: *"My reply is no."*

Q: *Will humanity ever colonize other planets?*
A: *"My reply is no."*

Q: *Will humanity destroy itself?*
A: *"No."*

Q: *Will something else destroy humanity?*
A: *"Yes."*

Q: *Is it possible to know what will de-*
   stroy humanity?
A: *"Without a doubt."*

Q: *Will a giant meteor destroy human-*
   ity?
A: *"It is certain."*

Q: *Do we have millions of years before*
   that happens?
A: *"As I see it, yes."*

Q: *Should we try to enjoy the time re-*
   maining as best we can?
A: *"Most likely."*

Q: *Is it time for a coffee break?*
A: *"Concentrate and ask again."*

Q: *Is ... it ... time ... for ... a ... coffee*
   ... break?
A: *"It is certain."*

Wordless Moments

WORDLESS MOMENTS

A chanter drones and pipes wail of life and love and
man's travail.

A serving tray remains balanced, quite
Impeccably and on the tilt of your hand
It seems to float toward the stage where
I sit on short riser stands; embracing a
Chanters drone and pipes that wail.
A long-forgotten lamentation of life
Embracing and devouring you with
A soulful, ravenous hunger... I harvest

The green that flows through veins al-
lowing
These tearful notes to bend in the wind
and
Caress your cheeks, hiding beneath the
Silken strands of your hair; imagined
between
My fingers that only triple-stop
To momentarily feign ignorance of
The impish sparkle in your laughing
eyes
As you renew the dew of life's tempta-
tions.

There is a closeness in this room
And it … encourages a kinship of sorts.
A remembrance, through the mists of
       time
Of visages… places described in verse
       from
Old to young; a wheel rolling, turning
Through history that pauses briefly at
       each
House to drink from the cup that is the
Cherished communion; the spirit of the
       age.

The evening grows plump and full as
Patrons slump and amble street bound
       in a sort of
Blessed serenity toward nesting
Lofts tinkered together; emerald tran-
       soms…
An effective time-tested styling
That relaxes purse and passion inher-
       ited
Through many repressed generations.

Oh what have we done dear, sweet
       Molly!?
The garden gate is flung open wide and
       I

For one, tremble at the mere sight of
you
Knowing a shortness of breath and
quickness of
Heart that comes in the final gasps
Of one succumbing to victimless drown-
ing.

Into the depths of your dark-pool eyes...
Water of the night blooming rose, sent
quietly
Upon fragrant zephyr breeze, to stir
The leaves that surround my wistful
desire.

But your hallowed wisdom precedes
Timeless ardour and my ignorance of
Such matters and a gentle chide de-
fends
Aptly against such men and their col-
lective
Common ignorance; for you are the
Embodiment of what is, yet may never
Be - unless you too would surrender
All for a brief glimpse of love - love as
perfect
As we poor mortals may yet attain.

We remain, warm finger tips touching

And our heart beats paused, drifting in
the time and
Space between eternities; in pious
Contemplation of random, wordless
moments.

Stubborn

STUBBORN

When no agreement is possible...

You are the rock and
I the wind.
I must flow around you
on my journey, gently
whispering
goodbye.

I Me We and You

I ME WE AND YOU

I me we and you
all together .. in a small can of goo
up come the sails out go the rails
we row and stroke and it pours
and .. the oars are lost, bobbing away
like analogies at play.

So, in my day - I me we and you
tall, proud, time-covered .. as statues in
                    the park
and surly dogs at night that bark
at haversacks of little mints
everyone chosen, eaten at random
until, by the fall of roman columns
no more apples bobbing and so

it's just I me we and you.

Sad Ornamental Bookends

SAD ORNAMENTAL BOOKENDS

Beware all creatures down below
An elephant is dying, very slow

See, it has finally come to rest
See, where it has taken its last step

It's come at last, a favorite spot
Where the parching sun can reach it not

Where it may recall fond memories
Of earth and sky and trees with leaves

It sways back and forth, its skin hangs
*   down*
It's long trunk unpacked upon the
*   ground*

The shade of this tree must be the best
Where it's time is now, where it can
*   rest*

It stands and sways as it remembers
Tender shoots and rains of November

It sways here, upon this dusty ground

Casting its shadow, making no sound

It's family gatherers round it now
Touching gently, pillared leg or brow

A knee buckles, it begins to kneel
No silver church bells are heard to peal

Where it has taken its final step
They gather round now, to see it rest

Beware all creatures down below
An elephant is dying, very slow

The Downside of Up

THE DOWNSIDE OF UP

The downside
of UP
is
The Downside

I wonder too much
and
I think too little
Time to
Rosin up the bow

and
Play a little fiddle

The upside
of DOWN
is
The Upside

There's a Hole in Your Ego

THERE'S A HOLE IN YOUR EGO

I see there's a hole in your ego
Where the sun shines through,
Upon sunny pastoral scenes,
Quite a lovely view.

But it contrasts with the overcast,
The clouds of the past where
Our thunder rumbles and
our lightning Scenes flash fast, striking

Outcropping's of memory mountains,
Silhouettes, emotions -
Rugged and vast they shelter a small
            soul's
                Wilderness-dark crevasse.

Reach out to me, I to you, perhaps
We can abide there too...
But prefer that sunny, grassy sward
Where flowers of poems grow

... gently from your words.

Aloof

ALOOF

You are... aloof, beautiful and irre-
sistible
I sing your praises in my mind but at
no time
Do I utter a sound you might detect.
Still, you come to me, after I have lost
all hope.

Throwing your elegantly proud head to
one side
Taking a place near, turning down a
well-groomed ear.
Perhaps a token of feigned disregard
Just before curling beneath my chin
and whiskers.

There you begin a purring rhythm that
calms the storms
And melts away those nervous cares of
dark days
That remind of ill times manifest
From unbecoming things; strange and
gray and gloomy.

With a distant proximity our thoughts
wander
In and out of that soothing, common
space where time
Is just a word that seeks to find mean-
ing
Beyond you - aloof, beautiful and irre-
sistible.

Fickle

FICKLE

sounds, random words in tandem
a'going where the winds blow
strands of hair, birds abandon
the nest that's lost its glow

oh cattle lowing, from where you call,
do you see the garden wall

do you see the hillock high, there, upon
which the farmer sighs
and wonders where thou art as the sun
goes down and fills his heart
with dread and causes such sturdy
frown etched upon his aged
brow

swallows quickly dart about
lambs bleating for shelter
as young dogs and children shout
running helter skelter

in the dusk, the candle glowing through
windowed light, inside show-
ing
each before the table, chair, and kettle
fire... all hands folded, heads
bowed low
such is taught and so rustic prayer,
humble thoughts sent smartly
rowing
up the rail to catch a breeze that
tickles... none shall ever know

which way this clay does she play
with hammer or curved sickle
a lovers oath sworn that day
who knew a love so fickle

Chapter 38

Stories

City Rabbit and Country Rabbit

Once there were two little rabbits. One was born in a thick hedge, inside a park within a city. The other was born in a patch of large brush beside a farmer's field in the country.

Each little rabbit dreamed big rabbit dreams. City rabbit dreamed of going to the other side of the large hill in the middle of the park. Country rabbit dreamed of what might be inside the middle of the farmer's field. Each dreamed of something beyond home. But, it is hard to dream about things one has never seen before so each little rabbit decided that, one day, they would go where they had never been before.

The day for adventure came to each little rabbit; as it always does.

... City rabbit loped over the hill inside the city park and saw... giant things. They were nothing like rabbits. There were so very tall and big and they walked on two very long legs instead of hopping near the ground like rabbits. City rabbit saw four-legged things too; much bigger than rabbits and with long pink tongues and long, sharp white teeth. It thought that they could run fast... faster than the the tall, two-legged things but not as fast as a rabbit.

... Country rabbit watched carefully from its hiding place inside the brush beside the farmer's field. It sniffed the air for smells of large, four-legged things and searched the sky for large flying things. These things liked to chase rabbits. Sometimes they caught them too and took them away; then they didn't come home. So country rabbit watched and waited and when it seemed that there was nothing in the wind or in the sky it loped into the farmer's field. The grass was tall and there were clumps of sweet clover to nibble on. Country rabbit continued to sniff the air and watch the sky and nibble on clover and sweet grass.

... Meanwhile, city rabbit was loping around the large hill in the center of the park when it came upon a large, brown thing that smelled like wood but wasn't a tree. Inside there were other smells too and green things that seemed good to eat. He nibbled a bit from one and it was delicious! City rabbit had never eaten lettuce before... or carrots or cabbage. City rabbit had discovered a box of garden things. How it came to be there we do not know but we do know that city rabbit was enjoying nibbling so much that it did not notice when the top of the box shut suddenly. It was now dark but the box was moving. City rabbit stopped eating. City rabbit could not see a way to hop out of the box so it was afraid and its heart beat very fast.

... The sun was rising higher in the sky where country rabbit sat nibbling. Its ears turned this way and that, listening to the sounds of the farmer's field. There were sounds of birds and the wind in the grass and something else. A low rumbling in the distance like thunder before it rains; but not thunder. Country rabbit thought about this new sound and as it chewed sweet grass the sound became louder and louder. Country rabbit stopped nibbling and sat up as tall as it could. Its ears poked up above the clover and its large black eyes saw something coming toward it from the far side of the field. It was a large red thing that sounded like distant, rolling thunder. As it came closer it made strange, loud clacking sounds and dark gray smoke puffed from its head. The tall grass fell on each side of it as it rolled toward where country rabbit stood, frozen, with its heart racing.

... City rabbit could feel the box that carried it move up and down. Strange new sounds came to its ears from outside. Inside the box, sitting in the dark, it began to shake and its heart beat even faster. After a short time, that seemed a very long time, the box stopped moving. Something outside the box began to make loud sniffing sounds and to scratch at the lid of the box. Suddenly, the box tipped over and the lid flew open. City rabbit did not hesitate but jumped out of the box and began to run. It ran across a dark gray expanse toward the hill at center of the park. As it came to the grass at the edge of the park it took one final leap and near the end of its leap something very large, noisy and hard struck its hind legs, spinning it in the air. City rabbit landed in the grass and tumbled under a large hedge. One of its legs hurt badly. So, it loped in small little steps, deeper into the hedge where it was darkest. There it rested for a time.

... In the farmer's field a thing, louder than thunder, came ever closer to country rabbit. At some moment, known only to those rabbits that have become frozen with fear, a spark of courage lit a fire inside and it began to leap in large, high jumps toward the edge of the field. It raced in front of the falling grass and with one final leap escaped into the fence row and the brush that was its home. But country rabbit had not jumped high enough or fast enough. Bright drops of blood fell from its foot where three little toes used to be. It hopped through the brush to its home. There it sat in pain, thinking of the farmer's field and its day of adventure. After a while, although missing its toes, the pain went away. Time passed and it lived a long time for a rabbit. But, even though it often dreamed of the sweet grass and clover, it never again went into the farmer's field.

... In the city the sun had set and the park was deserted and quiet. Moonlight appeared upon the grassy hill. City rabbit limped across the cool grass. From the dark cover of trees it eventually found its way home into the bushes. Soon its leg healed but it always had a little limp from that time forward. Sometimes it remembered the other side of the hill and the box. But it never again thought to visit the other side of the hill and so it stayed near its home at the edge of the park and there it lived, as happy as any rabbit can be with its family, for the rest of its natural life.

... Brave little rabbits who seek adventure often find it and may have many things to remember and dream about; if they come home. The moral of this story, if there is one, is that every adventure has a price and we should always try to appreciate what we have but sometimes it takes an adventure to learn this and to understand it.

Joey Luck

Joey Luck

The winters are colder these days but its warm here inside the nightclub and the booze is good for a quick flash in the pants as long as you don't go outside and think it's going to keep you from freezing to death. Global Warming... sounds sort of like a bad joke to think that it's colder because the world is getting warmer. But what do I know? I just work here. I'm one of the bouncers here at Harvey's Place. I help to make sure the loud-mouth belligerents, the ones that are mean-tempered drunks, leave as quickly as possible. Usually though, I stand at the entrance looking all pretty and girly-girly; just inside the door with the big white neon rabbits on either side. Harvey.. giant rabbit.. get it? Never mind, you're probably too young. Anyway, it pays good and pretty soon, with any luck, I'll have my doctorate in Criminal Psychology. After that, maybe a steady job somewhere so I can start to pay off this mountain of student loans that keep piling up.

I was born thirty two years ago as 'Josephine Lucy Smith.' My dad was an old "I Love Lucy" nostalgic and 'Lucy' was a compromise between my parents and my mother's grandmother, 'Lucille Anna Maria Francesco.' At some point I must have asked my dad, the family historian and community college science teacher, about my name. That's when he told me the cute little story about how he and mom had fought or rather "discussed" what I should be named before I was born. By the way, my mom had earned her degree in sports medicine while working her way though college with, of all things, a boxing scholarship. He said that the name Lucille means light and then quickly added that it was too close in spelling to 'Lucilia', the name for a species of irridescent green blowfly; thus the compromise of 'Lucy.' Funny, how much I disliked the color green after that in favor of the bright reds of valentine hearts, blood, and as a trim for black satin.

When I was a kid my older brothers called me 'Josie' or sometimes 'Joey.' My younger brother, William was still learning to read and the first time he saw my name in print he pronounced 'Lucy' as 'Luky (/ˈləkē/).' He'd just learned the 'u' sound in "Mr. Squirrel's Nuts" so 'lucky' seemed right to him. My parents corrected him but he just couldn't seem to get it out of his head for a long time... probably something to do with the squirrel. At any rate it was good for a laugh. From then on everybody, family and friends, started calling me 'Josie Luck' or sometimes just 'Joey Luck.' As a nickname it stuck... good and tight. So, there you have it. That's why my friends all laugh and call me 'Joey Luck' or 'Joe Luck'; my enemies too... but they don't usually laugh. It seems I've got a lot of enemies these days. I can't imagine why.

Red Ivory

Did I mention that I was also minoring in Mathematics and Martial Arts? No? Sorry about that. It always seems to come as a shock to people that those subjects actually go quite well together. The martial arts keep you physically in shape and the psych is good for getting inside your opponents head; the math is good to... for figuring the odds that you're going to survive to fight again some day. It's also good for working the back rooms and pool halls that surround the campus; to pick up some extra money for groceries and such. You can meet some really interesting people in those kind of places and some really dangerous ones too.

It was still lightly snowing the night my math study group decided to knock off early and go shoot a couple of games of pool. We were having a great time until a couple of fur-faced guys in goth-drab, reeking of motor oil, pulled up chairs next to our table and started narrating the game action. Badly too I might add. After a few more beers disappeared into the brush patches under their big noses they really turned up the volume. At that point, I asked them to either 'turn it down a little' or 'shut up while I'm shooting' ... something like that. I'm sure we must have looked 'easy' and when the big one got up and spun me around hard while I was trying to gently stroke the cue ball I just had to show him how the 'monkey grabs the peach.' His knees wobbled a little before he rolled to the floor writhing in pain. The smaller one tried to bring his bottle into play but he had been a little too cocky in leaning back in his chair. That's not good for balance and a whack from the heavy end of my pool que sent it flying out from beneath him. His head hit the concrete floor with a sick little crack. I remember thinking that's probably going to leave a bump.

With a flood of adrenaline trying to commandeer my

common sense I resisted the urge to leave my heel marks tattooed in places where someone would notice. Fortunately my friends were anxious to leave and the management gave us their blessings to do so in the most ungracious fashion possible.

Back at my off-campus apartment I shook off the effects of the recent dirt-bag drama and decided to settle into a tub of warm suds and candles. I hated going to bed while I was all wound up. I was well up to my ears in warm water and bubbles and into an marvelous imaginary philosophical discussion between Leibniz's rationalism versus Koyre's metaphysics when my cell phone started to play one of its random ring tones, Beethoven's Fifth.

Feeling Lucky

It was my boyfriend, Vince. An image of him flashed into my mind as he said, "Hey Joey! How are you doing? I heard you had some fun at the pool hall tonight." He was a knockout, really. I've been told that I'm easy on the eyes but he's the kind of guy that can pull a girl's eyeball's right out of their sockets; a regular roman god in the flesh. Nice flesh too... a lot of it, in all the right places. "I'm doing OK, Vince. I'm over it now... just relaxing in the tub.", I said. "Do you care if I come over for a little bit? Just to make sure you're OK and all, you know.", he said. "I have training in the morning and an exhibition match in the afternoon so you can't stay long, OK?", I said. "Sure. No problem. I'll just stay a few minutes and then be on my way. See you in a few.", he said. I pressed the disconnect and placed the phone on the table beside the tub.

In a few more minutes I had rinsed, dried my hair and put on my silky red PJs and a large black plush bathrobe. Grabbing some homework I curled up on the couch and waited for Vince to arrive. I didn't have long to wait. He lives only a couple of blocks away. I jumped up to answer the apartment door as soft chimes sounded in the hallway. I'd learned a long time ago that you don't just open a door even if you think you know who's on the other side. I had the landlord remove the peephole thing too; they're worthless and let other people look back inside with another set of lenses.

Standing a little to one side I asked, "Who is it?" Vince's muffled voice replied from the other side, "It's me, Joey. Open up." The thick oak door creaked a little on it's antique hinges as I opened it slowly, still chained, to do a reality-check and see who was actually there. Vince has one of those voices that sounds a lot like other roman gods. I needed to make sure the right one was on the other side. It was. I unchained the door and he stepped in as I closed and secured the door once again.

"Hey, baby! You look great. How you feeling?", he said as he reached out to match my embrace. I placed my head on his shoulder and snuggled up into his neck as I said, "I'm fine. You know I can usually take care of myself. They were just a couple of Jimmy's twerps. No big deal. He'll smack their ears if he hears about how they were mouthing off to me. He likes the way I play poker you know." Vince grinned and said, "Yea, I've learned my lesson. Just friendly poker with you. But those rocks you bought with the pots you've won look good on you." I smiled and said, "Let's sit down. Move that stuff and I'll bring you something to drink. Just remember, I have to get to bed early... big day tomorrow." He smiled as he sat down in a corner of the couch and leaned up against a pile of pillows.

Returning from the kitchen I sat two glasses and a bottle of wine on the table, poured a bit in each and handed him a glass. "So, what have you been up to this week? I haven't seen you for days.", Vince rumbled. "The usual graduate classes and exams this week. Finals next. You know the drill by now. This is not the time for me to become distracted with my social life.", I purred. "Well, it's good that your friends are a bit easier to get information out of than you are otherwise I wouldn't have a clue what goes on in your life when I'm not around.", he said, grinning. "Oh! So, keeping tabs on me, huh? And now you're pumping my friends for information?", I shot back with an feigned expression of anger as I cuddled up close to him. "Are you sure you want to take the chance that someone that shouldn't will learn that you're hooked up with me?" He slipped a warm hand inside my bathrobe. "No problem there, Joey. You know, when I'm with you, I always feel lucky.", he said, softly, as his eyes closed and his lips found mine.

The Writers Cafe

This is just fiction (wink, grin.)
Prologue

We humans are not the only creatures that dream. It's just hard to prove it to people that have not given it much thought. However, there are a lot of people that would be more than willing to agree that their dog or cat or bird or fish dreams. We watch them and see them tremble in their sleep and we just know they're dreaming.

Over many thousands of years humans have developed associative bonds with their companion species. To our special friends we have granted certain anthropomorphic rights. For example, the right to feel what we are feeling, the right to think as we do and to see us as we truly are. If we have a certain philosophical outlook on life or a particular political leaning then we almost always assume, on some subliminal level, that they share the same views and sentiments as we do. Why is that?

Perhaps it's because we never really try talking to them. We never really attempt to communicate with them on any meaningful level. And, if we do, it's usually at the adult-child level or some other hierarchy where we assume ourselves to be at the top of the universe of all thought.

To help us get a better sense of this unique relationship let us imagine for a moment a person we shall call Marge. Let us imagine that Marge is having a "chat" with her four-legged companion. It might go something like this:

"Does momsy womsy's little pookie snookums want a treat?", said Marge. "Marge, I'm as round as beach ball. Why do you keep stuffing those things down me? You know I can't resist them! You're not trying to fatten me up so you can eat me are you?", thinks Pookie. "You're such a good pookie snookums!", says Marge. "Marge, if you knew what really happened to your new shoe you might not say that.", thinks Pookie. "Is that why you want to fatten me up and eat me? Because of a that stupid shoe?! Marge, you're an animal!"

Of course that's just a fantasy to illustrate a relationship that is almost always one-sided. What could these non-human creatures have to say to us that would be of any value or interest? After all, we are the superior species are we not?

Adrian

Adrian is awake, up and in the shower twenty minutes before the alarm goes off. It isn't unusual to wake up earlier than normal but this morning the air seems charged with a strange energy. An energy that flows through every muscle, synapse and neuron giving Adrian a momentum that is well beyond the norm.

Adrian is dressing quickly. The bus is coming soon and it doesn't wait. Adrian really likes to go to work because the job is very special. Adrian is one of the few employees that is paid to read. Paid to read and to dream... big dreams; and to imagine things that might be... in some way, of benefit to "the company". Adrian reads about many different things but mostly about things that appear in science fiction, fantasy and science journals. Prose and poetry are wonderful, useful too... anything that evokes emotion or seems of interest or in some way related to the company's mission. The company has many missions. The company is everywhere.

Adrian arrives at the office and settles into the large cushioned chair by the window. The one that overlooks the harbor. The assistant staff has placed a cup of coffee, juice, a plain bagel and some bland nutrient spread on a nearby coffee table. It's enough to last until lunch. There is a slight grey-blue overcast to the sky and a cool drizzle of rain runs down the outside of the smoky window glass. Perfect reading weather. Perfect for dreaming with eyes and mind wide open. This place, this corner office - it's well off the main route of normal foot traffic and there are few distractions. It's a good place to read... a good place to resonate with the mind of "the author" dujour.

Adrian knows that some of the authors are special but doesn't know exactly why. There's only "the theory" to act as guide; to help in the sifting, winnowing and ultimate selection of items that will be entered into the report. It's a special report. One that is read by only a few highly-placed people in the company. They never provide any feedback. But that doesn't matter. The pay check and benefits are very generous and provide a base of motivation for "the work." It's good that they don't know - Adrian would probably do the work for free. Adrian really likes to read and, after all, it is a very intriguing theory.

A theory that seems to bear fruit in the most unusual places. A fruit born of thoughts and ideas and concepts that are both unique and connected by a commonality that is measurably significant. It is this significance, a scientific tour du force confirmed by a select group of scientists, mathematicians as well a cloud of computers that provide the basis for the theory - and the work. But, it is Adrian's input, the daydreams, the insights, the unexplainable mental connectives that guide the process beyond mere attribute-classified selection.

Some have tried to explain the success of the theory

by using esoteric concepts such as sixth sense, spooky action-at-a-distance or quantum entanglement. But those big words, those big ideas have yet to produce any results like that of Adrian, "the reader."

The Theory

Quickly scanning and selecting several items from the pile of books and papers on the coffee table Adrian sets them aside while logging into the company computer; a vast network of people, machines and systems that make the work feasible as well as very lucrative. Adrian begins each morning by reviewing the postings within a circle of online acquaintances affectionately known as "the friends." The friends are writers - authors of strange and ragged verse, unusual stories, and written fragments of ideas, thoughts and emotions; most imaginary, some real.

The theory assigns only a superficial weighting between input that may be tagged as imaginary or real. It is the thoughts of the reader that provide the distinctions, the attributes that provide the essential factors that, when fed into formulas of mind-numbing complexity, yield the distilled essence of "the message." And the message is no less than the greatest oxymoron ever encountered. A message of such complex simplicity that most reject it out-of-hand as pure nonsense upon first reading. Some speculate that the human mind is pre-wired to think such thoughts. Thoughts such as the ones that are the essential components that comprise snippets of the message. In the theory, the message is said to resonate within the minds of singular individuals. Much in the same manner and as simply as a string vibrates when plucked by the hand of a musician. It is as though mind and instrument have each evolved and been created for the sole purpose of receiving the message. Collectively they are referred to as "the receiver."

Adrian recalls the many notable receivers identified by the theory in just the past century: Jules Verne, Samuel Clemens, E.E. Doc Smith, Arthur C. Clark, Robert A. Heinlien, Kim Stanley Robinson, Marion Zimmer Bradley, Julian May, J. R. R. Tolkien, Andre Norton, Stanley Kubrik, William Blake, Louisa May Alcott, Percy Byshee Shelly, John Keats... the list goes on and on. There is always a pool of receivers. They are self-renewing, self-perpetuating and they occur throughout all of recorded history; and perhaps, some not yet recorded or long forgotten. The antikythera mechanism comes to mind.

In the theory, the receiver is said to have the property of self-assembly. Adrian ponders this and envisions the human mind evolving over time into a form and structure that eventually is able to resonate with certain components of the message. But the receiver is not a single thing, not a single organism but rather a collective of individuals, of minds or mind-components that each provide certain bits of data, parts of the message, that when assembled in the correct order become a report.

There is also the polar opposite. If there is a receiver then it is reasonable to assume that there should also be a sender or a plurality of senders. But the essence of the sender is ephemeral and yet all-encompassing. It stubbornly refuses quantification or classification and can be described only in broad stokes of the brush, in general terms at best. It is the nature of "the sender" that is the most perplexing component of the theory. That a sender exists is irrefutable because the message exists but as to its source and essence there can be only wild speculation. Such localization and confirmation is beyond the current state of the theory.

The Work

As the day unfolds, Adrian selects certain key concepts and mentally compares them to similar ones by other authors, even though they may be stated in dramatically different fashion. It is this perception, this resonance of the color and shape and form of thought that permits an n-dimensional structure to form in the mind of the reader; in Adrian's mind. Taken individually they are of little concern. But to Adrian it is noteworthy that an author in one period in history conceives of a unique and here-to-fore unstated concept such as the vibration of mind. A vibration that can span any physical distance instantaneously. Does such an ancient thought overlap or evoke a resonance with the concept of quantum entanglement in the physics of this age? It does and Adrian makes a note of the relationship and inputs it into the system. The theory will determine if it is significant and include it in a report if there are sufficient occurrences within the existing corpus of humanity's authorial output. Each report contributes to the message as humanity tries, desperately at times, to fit the pieces of the puzzle together. There is a sense of urgency. Everyone feels it at some level. It is akin to the strange energy that pulled Adrian out of bed well before the normal time today.

Relaxing in the chair Adrian stares out the window for a moment, looking at nothing in particular. Attention wandering back into the room, a strange feeling draws Adrian's gaze upward where a small spider is vibrating in its web in a corner of the ceiling. A small thrill of electricity ensues as each corner of the room reveals a similar sight. Spiders in each one. Each vibrating in unison with the other. What are the odds? Why are they doing this? As Adrian thinks the final question each spider stops vibrating simultaneously. Another electric thrill courses through Adrian's body after looking at a particular spider and thinking, "Hello!" only to have the chosen spider seemingly respond with a frantic gyration and then stop. Each spider responds in exactly the same way to the same thought as if reading Adrian's mind. It is a particularly odd occurrence. One worthy of note and entry into the system.

Unknown to Adrian, the system produce a special report. The report contains a section providing statistics of significance correlating descriptions of mental communications between human and non-human life forms as noted by various authors over several thousand years. Language-specific words, phrases, descriptions, and contexts are processed by using the theory. They are distilled into several of the most probable interpretations. Each interpretation is considered and selected by upper-echelon readers that select one or more for inclusion into the message. The message is growing. The message is... alarming. It is about us. It is to us. The message asks if we are listening. It asks if we are awake?

Dreamland

Adrian is tired after the bus ride home. The energy of the morning is gone. It is dark. It is late and the bed is soft and inviting. Eyes close and there is a rush and jumble of thoughts and voices that appear within Adrian's mind. Swashes of color and sound become scenes and images; of people, places and things. Some familiar, some so strange as to defy description. In that moment before darkness overtakes the mind a single image, a single thought reaches out over vast distances without the perception of time. Adrian is standing on an alien landscape and there too stands a giant spider that is at least Adrian's own height. The spider moves closer and extends a pedipalp toward Adrian's shoulder. A thought resonates in the mind commingled with a sense of fear and well-being, a salutation of greeting and friendship, "I will eat you when you die." It is an alien thought borne of an alien mind existing within an alien culture, an alien civilization... and it shocks Adrian as no other thought has ever done before. The message, the greeting of friendship... Adrian drifts motionless into the mystery of dreams.

Three Candles

Believe it or not it is warm and sunny for a few days
out of the year in New Hampshire. The warmth and sun
are good for growing things. Trees, flowers, gardens, grass..
especially the grass. There are all kinds of grass but the
kind that grows in New Hampshire is usually of two kinds;
native and nursery grown. Both are adored and hated.
Adored by those that enjoy the sight of a verdant green
sward in summer and hated by those unfortunate ones that
must keep them trimmed in accordance with the imagina-
tions and specifications drawn up by the village select men
and women. The same elected officials that preside over
such things in their centuries old black and white meeting
places with the unfailing regularity of precision clockwork.
Some call them the keepers of the Puritan flame while se-
cretly espousing sentiment that alludes to a feeble legacy
of the English gentry; a localized, self-appointed royalty
with altogether too much idle time on their hands - this
according to some.

From belt line orbit the butt of a smoking cigarette
spiraled through the muggy summer atmosphere onto the
black asphalt below producing an ejecta of orange sparks
and gray ash. Scott Ridley crushed out the remaining em-
bers with the worn edge of a hiking boot as he brushed
damp tawny curls from the aquamarine eyes set deeply
into his white freckled face. With a vacant stare he followed
the movements of two people, a boy and a girl, crossing the
high school parking lot. Arm-in-arm they ambled toward
him where he stood with arms folded on his chest, leaning
against an old rust-red pickup truck. It should have been a

new truck. He had mowed a lot of grass to save up for one. That's what his dad had promised. But he didn't make the football playoffs. Now in his last year of high school he had become familiar with another variety of grass and had been summarily kicked off the team after the coach had discovered him and his buddies smoking it in the broom closet beside the boy's locker room.

"Hey, Scott!", shouted Justin. "Don't look so pissed. We're only a little bit late. Caley had to talk with her band teacher about playing at the game this weekend." Caley smiled warmly as they approached Scott and said, "Hi, Scott. It' nice to see you again. Where have you been lately? Are you coming to the dance after the game this weekend?"

"Probably not but I have some ideas for after the dance, if you're interested.", said Scott.

"What kind of ideas are we talking about?", said Justin.

"There's that old deserted cabin up by the lake. I thought you guys might want to go up there after the dance and spend the night.. hang out for a bit, catch up, you know.", said Scott. "It's been a long time since we were there and its cool by the lake at night; especially when its so hot this time of year. It might be fun.. what do you think?"

"I told my parents that we were going to stay at Julia's house after the dance.", said Caley.

"That's right.", said Justin. "Julia's parents have it worked out with our folks. We're all going to watch some old movies in the basement then have breakfast and then go home."

"Well, you could still do that. You'ld just be a little bit later than expected, right?", said Scott. A pouty look beginning to appear on his face.

"I suppose we could..", said Caley. "As long as we don't stay too long at the lake cabin. What do you think Justin?"

"Yea, I suppose so. But we'll need to be back in time for at least one old movie and breakfast. Can't miss the best meal of the day. Julia's mom makes some great pancakes you know!", said Justin, jokingly.

History is a big part of the ambiance that is New England and New Hampshire is blessed with it in abundance. It instills a respect for things past in the people that grow up or live there for a period of time. Perhaps it was that unconscious sense of history that caused Scott to review in his mind some chapters from their early school days. The days when he and Justin had vied for the attention and hand of the young Caley. Caley had been very impartial when they were young, fawning over them both as equitably as possible with smiles, conversation and childhood games. But eventually the games were put aside as nature brought irresistible forces to bear upon their bodies. The laws of attraction remained a mystery to Scott. All he could remember of this particular history was that Caley had chosen Justin. It had hurt him with a new kind of pain. One that he tried to endure but one that ultimately led to his associations with questionable friends; older boys, men really, that only feigned friendship in return for his help as an unwitting pawn in their dark ambitions to rule the backwaters of New Hampshire, much as their cronies did in the larger cities of Boston and New York.

A wise man once said that nobody is born hating another. If that's true then hating is learned. But for hatred to grow it must be cultivated and Scott had learned the art of cultivating hatred. Sometimes he wasn't even aware of it. It became second nature to him; to help distribute the tokens of undeniably pleasurable servitude to the young, the rebellious, the unsuspecting. Those whose parents both worked or habitually stayed out late and permitted the mass media to supplement their meager parenting skills. His pain found some aberrant release in this hatred, this anti-love that had filled his heart since that time when he had been rejected. Rejected more times than he cared to recall; history be damn.

...

"It's nice up here. It brings back lots of memories.", said Caley as she stood beside the lake shore with Justin and Scott on either side of her. Though the waters were dark, the stars were bright and the breeze moving across the lake was cool and refreshing. She remembered, long ago, idly teasing small pebbles into the water and watching as the low rays of a golden sunset revealed lake trout rushing to gulp and then spit them out in disgust. "Remember when we were kids and we would come up here in the summer with our folks?", said Caley.

"Yea, that was a long time ago.", said Scott.

"Not so long.. we're not that old.", smiled Justin. "You make it sound like we're fourty; ancient or something."

"Whatever..", said Scott. "Say, let's go inside. I brought some snacks, drinks and other stuff."

"OK.", said Caley. "What did you bring?"

"Only your favorite.. S'mours.", smirked Scott. "You still like those don't you?"

"Sure do!", said Caley. "Let's go inside Justin."

Once inside, Justin started a fire in the old stone fire-
place. Caley set out and lit three red candles that she had
brought just for the occasion, placing them well in front of
the fire but still on the stones. Sharpened sticks served to
impale the marshmallows and soon the delicate aroma of
graham crackers, chocolate and melted marshmallow filled
the old cabin's main room. Sitting on sleeping blankets
they chatted about everything and nothing in particular.
After a while, Scott pulled out something from his back-
pack and set it in front of them.

"I've got to get going. Got some stuff to do but here's
something to end the evening with.. something to remember me by.", said Scott as he rose to his feet, grabbed his
backpack and walked out the door. The sound of his old
truck clawing its way down the gravel road faded away
leaving only the occasional sneeze or snap of the dieing fire.

"What did Scott leave us.. what is that stuff, Justin?",
asked Caley.

"Looks like a couple of joints." said Justin. "Do you want
to smoke them?"

"I haven't smoked anything since we were kids!", giggled
Caley. "Do you remember? We got caught and grounded
for a month."

"Yes, I remember.", grinned Justin. "I doubt we would
get caught up here. We'll be leaving in another hour or
two. Plenty of time to get straight, right?"

In due time they had settled into the sleeping bag.
Justin's arms surrounded his dear Caley, pulling her close,
their heads propped up on the old pillows they had
brought.

Staring into the candles, Caley said, "Justin, do you love me?"

"I think.. I know I do.", said Justin.

"I know you do too. I just wanted to hear you say it again.", said Caley as she snuggled even closer allowing his hand to find her bare stomach. She noted the strength, the warmth of it even as a warm glow filled her body from head to toe. She stared at the fire, the candles, and drifted off as the darkness enfolded her consciousness.

Justin awoke to the sound of something rustling in the old juniper tree outside the cabin. Probably an owl or some other bird thought Justin. The last red candle flickered. It's flame heaving between bright and dim, as though gasping to sustain itself upon the remnants of the drowning wick. He leaned over and kissed Caley's exposed shoulder. His lips met with the coolness of the night. He reached up and softly brushed the hair from the back of Caley's neck and then kissed it gently. It too, oddly cool. His hand slipped beneath the cover of the sleeping blanket, seeking the warm flesh of her exposed stomach. Cold. Too cold.

"Caley?", he whispered. Nothing. Raising himself upon one elbow he spoke with rising concern, "Caley? Answer me..", said Justin. Gently he rolled her toward him. Her eyes were open.. looking up at him.. no, not him.. looking at.. nothing.

Justin stared in a horror of disbelief at Caley's vacant stare, that angelic face that he so dearly loved. The flame of the last red candle, heaved one final gasp of light and then there was only darkness.

Index

A River Lies Between Us,
    254
abstraction, 195
activism, 27
addiction, 158
adieu, 15
adornment, 148, 224
adventure, 72
affirmation, 181
alacrity, 75
alien, 42, 44, 117
allegorical, 69, 151, 186
allegory, 50
allusion, 25, 175
alone, 40
Aloof, 276
amalgam, 78
ambiguity, 40
amulet, 78
angels, 29, 31
angst, 14

anguish, 10
anthropomorphic, 79
antithesis, 224
apologies, 79
archaic, 217
arrogant, 24
articulation, 211
assimilation, 10
atonement, 47
attraction, 219
audience, 27
avatar, 118

babble, 41
bacteria, 222
bandage, 207
bardo, 93
basket, 95
battle, 47
beach, 145
bear, 215

beasts, 31
beautiful, 79, 94
beauty, 4, 43
beer, 94
beetles, 214
bell, 167
birthday, 32
bleed, 207
blind, 78
bliss, 133, 194
blood, 210
bloom, 180
blossom, 205
bottle, 78
brain, 53
brainfluff, 209
bravery, 157
breeze, 9
brow, 78
brusque, 211
bucket, 94
butterfly, 80, 83

California
    Capistrano, 76
    Long Beach, 42
    San Diego, 204
    Santa Cruz, 163
campfire, 31
candles, 27
canvas, 216

Caravaggio, 206
caricature, 186
catharsis, 118
chalkboard, 157
change, 187
Changes, 233
character, 45, 205, 212
charm, 77
cheer, 31
child, 100
children, 50, 155
Christmas, 19
circle, 171
City Rabbit and Country
            Rabbit, 281
civility, 44
clock, 180, 189
clouds, 9
clown, 31
cobweb, 224
coffee, 20, 185, 215
color, 78, 174, 207, 216
comedy, 152
commentary, 3
commiserate, 223
commiseration, 4
commitment, 27
communicate, 9
commutation, 24
companionship, 14
compassion, 105

complexity, 200
compliment, 72, 178
comprehension, 56
compromise, 20
conflict, 31
conflicted, 100
confusion, 73, 176
consciousness, 78
    stream-of, 4, 17
consideration, 154
consternation, 225
contemplate, 20
    contemplations, 20
contemplation, 53, 175
cookbook, 19
courage, 63
courageous, 57
coy, 211
creature
    of the abyss, 11
creepy, 26
crimson, 192
critic, 210
critique, 3
crystal, 66

dance, 19
dark, 47
Dark Love Burning, 251
darkness, 37
darwinism, 76

death, 20
debate, 195
Democrat, 210
demon, 24, 90
depravity, 140
depression, 52, 62
desert, 30
desire, 207
desolate, 32
despair, 3, 25, 200
    harmonies of, 10
desperation, 62
despondent, 32
destiny, 38
determinism, 187
dimesnsion
    3-dimensional, 20
dinosaur, 125
dog, 100, 120
dogma, 90
doldrums, 76
dolphin, 200
doormat, 90
doubt, 183
drama, 193
dreadnought, 187
dream, 175
    dreamer, 20
drink, 83
du jour, 11
dust, 69, 83, 131

earthworm, 176
eccentricity, 20
eclipse, 83
ego, 39
Eight Ball, 263
elephant, 32
elliptical, 174, 188
Elmo
    Tickle-me-Elmo,
        209
embarrass, 88
emotion, 15, 44, 65, 102,
    212
empathic, 200
empathy, 14
Empty Wells, 243
enemy, 27
enigmatic, 33
entropy, 196
epiphany, 77
equality, 198
equilibrium, 195
espresso, 153
ethereal, 184, 213
everything
    fit to publish, 40
    that lives dies, 38
evil, 39
exacerbation, 24
existence, 19, 43, 95, 101,
    134, 140

existential, 127
expectation, 102
    expectations, 20
expectations, 203
experience, 73, 78
explorer, 81
extrapolation, 76
extravagance, 30
eyes, 26

Face, 29
fantasy, 49, 64, 76, 182
fellowship, 26
female, 5
Fickle, 277
flag, 192
flesh, 23, 46, 96
flower, 66, 107, 171, 180,
    207
fluid, 179
foible
    human, 79
Forniclaise, 242
fractal, 219
Friends, 29
friendship, 73
frog, 187
fruit, 154
future, 29

gardening, 84
ghost, 19

glass, 78, 102, 121, 206
glimpse, 104
gloomy, 32, 84
goddess, 94
gods, 47, 95
Godzilla, 37
Graduation Day, 237
grammar, 89
grandeur, 213
gravity, 15, 55, 219
green, 78
grief, 40
grumpy, 40
guidance, 31
guitar, 26

happy, 73
harmony, 20, 95
hat, 46
hate, 181
heart, 27, 30, 41, 62, 77,
        120, 180, 207
Heaven, 31
hell, 65
hobbit, 106
hole
        There's a Hole in
        Your Ego, 275
homework, 206
hope, 181
hopeful, 73, 144

human, 38, 43, 130, 131,
        187
hypnotic, 72

I Me We and You, 272
ice, 216
idealism, 198
ignorance, 170
illusion, 20, 169, 198
imagery, 88, 96
imagination, 18, 46, 82,
        125, 194
immortality, 152
impression, 73
indecision, 73
industrial, 90
ingenious, 75
injustice, 199
ink, 215
innocence, 25
innocent, 81
inorganic, 186
insanity, 141
insomniac, 82
inspiration, 65, 75, 94
intellect, 176
intense, 207
interpretation, 79
intoxication, 216
introspection, 73
irony, 96, 199

jelly, 119
Jesus, 90
Joey Luck, 285
journey, 46, 69, 138
judge, 180
judgment, 124
juxtaposition, 212

kabuki, 117
Karma, 33
knowledge, 107

label, 156
labor, 30
lament, 15
lamentation, 109
landscape, 219
latin
    quid pro quo, 40
laughter, 137
laundry, 99
legacy, 91
life, 70, 77
    perceptions of, 10
    river of, 205
light, 65
linguistics, 187
liturgy, 209
loneliness, 62
Lost Cargo, 248
love, 14, 25, 31, 39–41,
        43, 72, 79, 114,
        115, 181, 191,
        218
    Love Circles, 256
    Silly Love Songs, 58

Machiavelli, 19
machine, 93
magic, 66, 112, 215
magnetic, 91, 103
Magnetic Poetry, 236
magyk, 47
male, 5
maxim, 27
meditation, 18
melancholy, 10, 52
memories, 39, 99
memory, 93, 127, 133
metaphor, 25, 69, 151,
        216
meteor, 37
metronome, 209
microscope, 100
mind, 23, 26, 46, 65, 161
    non-human, 195
minions, 187
mirror, 32
Mississippi, 186
mistakes, 206
mnemonic, 132
modesty, 203
monopole, 108

montage, 95
moon, 17, 64, 77, 127, 165
    moonbeams, 51
    struck, 15
    The Moon Is Full, 246
moonlight, 145
morality, 13, 23
moss, 219
Mothra, 37
mourning, 166
mouse, 72, 217
movies, 18
mystery, 46, 112
myth, 204

nature, 32
noodles, 79
Nostradamus, 19
nuance, 96

observation, 77
    observations, 20
ocean, 31, 66, 168, 170, 181, 192
octopus, 126
ominous, 88, 89
omniscient, 141
On Education, 241
On Sunday Drives, 244
optimism, 76

organic, 186

palette, 41
Pandora, 99
panoply, 224
pantheon, 77
pants, 183
paradigm, 227
paramount, 79
passion, 95, 133
pastoral, 89
pathos, 96
Pencil Masts, 261
pendulum, 72
penguin, 215
people
    saucer, 204
perception, 55
permutations, 50
perseverance, 225
perspective, 205, 221
perspiration, 25
philosophy
    philosophical, 18
phoenix, 64
pigtails, 33
pity, 189
planet, 222
plethora, 212
poetry, 3
poignant, 129

Polished Pieces, 235
pomposity, 33
poppies, 14
    gravity, 14
    provocation, 14
    sentiment, 14
    violence, 14
poppy, 194
posterity, 199
practice, 231
pray, 29
prayer, 185
prayers, 58
precocious, 102
predilection, 33
pretzel, 100
prey, 29
primeval, 50
priorities, 161
prize, 103
profanity, 186
protagonist, 57, 212
provocative, 44
psyche, 58, 89
psycho-mind-babble, 210
purge, 227

quintessential, 217
quiz
    multiple-choice, 30
Quotes, 56

rabbits, 71
rage, 26
rain, 10
    abyss, 10
    cello, 10
ramiparous, 84
ramparts, 199
random, 69, 79, 195
rationality, 10
Raven, 32, 65
reader, 46
Reading, 245
reality, 43, 76, 206
recipe, 19
reconstitute, 227
reflection, 46, 168
    silent, 11
reincarnation, 140
relationship, 101
Remorse, 243
remorse, 181
reply, 12
Republican, 210
resonance, 200
resplendent, 34
retreat, 174
review, 3, 231
    art-of, 4
riddle, 161
ring, 220
river, 152

roaches, 61
rocket, 93
romance, 13
rorschach, 76
roses
    chocolate, 31

Sad Ornamental Book-
    ends, 273
sadness, 95
Sailing San Diego, 234
sailor, 23, 77
salmon, 151
samba, 19
sarcasm, 70
satellite, 126
Saturn, 223
scenery, 44, 160
sea, 37, 72
seaweed, 170
secrets, 47
seductive, 88
sense, 31, 38, 50
sentiment, 109, 112
sequin, 195
serendipitous, 88
shadow, 65
    shadows, 19
sharp, 206
ship, 106
silence, 90

silhouette, 30, 171
sin, 47
sleep, 146, 162
smile, 177
snakes, 29
society, 182, 198
solace, 198
solution, 199
sorrow, 181, 191
soul, 9, 23, 72, 131, 180
sound, 219
spectrum, 173
sphere, 20, 206
spider, 219
spirit, 19, 84
spooky, 26
spoon, 95
spoonful, 193
sprocket, 93
St. Goodbye
    The Destiny of, 236
star, 108
starfish, 95
starlight, 131
Stick Bang Pow, 259
sticks, 153
stone, 194
story, 45
strategy, 206
strawberry, 95
Stubborn, 271

subatomic, 223
success, 147
suicide, 159
Summer, 71
summer, 76
sun, 43, 218
sunbeam, 183
sunlight, 108
sunset, 160
sunshine, 34
surreal, 114, 169
swallow, 76
swamp, 30
symbol, 41
symbolic, 187
symbolism, 5
symmetry, 129
sympathy, 207
symphony, 102
syncopation, 141

tapestry, 88
Tarot, 29
tavern, 94
tears, 66
telepathic, 31
tetrahedral, 144
texture, 78
The
      The Moon Is Full, 246

The Reading Room, 249
The Visit, 253
The Writers Cafe, 290
The Downside of Up, 274
The Voice Inside, 237
thematic, 4
thingamabobs, 188
thought, 46, 127, 140
Three Candles, 299
time, 131, 147
toast, 40
toga, 95
toil, 30
tolerance, 105
tomatoes, 207
tomb, 89
tourists, 13
tradition, 204
tragic, 26
train, 44
transcendental, 209
transformation, 70
transmogrify, 187
treasure, 188
trees, 9, 27
truth, 38, 39, 206
tsunami, 37
turmoil, 32
twisted, 49

unicorn, 34
universe, 12, 26, 62, 64,
        129

vegetable, 217
vibration, 9, 26
vignette, 134
vignettes, 79
vineyard, 124
volcano, 199
Voynich, 99

water, 70, 83, 116, 119
weather, 76, 135
weave, 109
whim, 147
whimsy, 34
whisper, 174
Whispers, 30
wind, 31
winter, 144
Winter Sleep, 247
wisdom, 23, 49, 200
woman, 217
Wordless Moments, 268
words, 33, 66
world, 134
worm, 14, 89, 118
writer, 81